COOKING FOR KIDS WITH CANCER

A parent's crash course on food and flavor during and after your child's cancer treatment.

By Chef Ryan Callahan

Copyright 2016 Ryan Callahan
All Rights Reserved
Published by Callahan Publishing

ISBN -13: 978-1534966314
ISBN-10: 1534966315

First Edition 2016

For more information and other books, please visit:
www.cookingforchemo.org

www.callahanpublishing.com

Table of Contents

WHAT YOU NEED TO KNOW BEFORE YOU BEGIN

2

Hello! Thank you so much for picking up a copy of *Cooking for Kids with Cancer!* My name is Chef Ryan Callahan. I am the author of this book, *Cooking for Kids with Cancer.* I am also the author of the book, *Cooking for Chemo... and After!* This is my second book along the themes of cooking, nutrition, and coping with cancer. I wrote the Gourmand Award winning book, *Cooking for Chemo ...and After!*, based on my experiences as a caregiver and a Chef. From 2013 to 2014, I acted as my mother's primary caregiver as she battled breast cancer and multiple surgeries. I cooked every meal for her, took her to doctor's appointments, and acted in every last capacity to ensure her survival during her fight with cancer. It was during this time as her caregiver that I was able to develop these cooking techniques and culinary theories that make such a difference in the lives of cancer fighters every where.

This book, *Cooking for Kids with Cancer*, represents a culmination of years of culinary expertise, feedback from cancer fighters, and new techniques that I have learned while helping other cancer fighters around the globe. I never could have imagined the response that I would get for *Cooking for Chemo ...and After!* That book has now been given to cancer fighters not just in the United States where I am located, but in Europe, Canada, and Australia as well. So, it is with this new international understanding that we have added conversion charts in the back of the book for ingredient names, fluid measurements, weight measurements, and specialty measurements. I have made my best efforts to make this book as easy as possible to use. But, it is not perfect. If you are unfamiliar with an ingredient or measurement, simply search the internet and learn more about it.

I undertook the writing of this book as a response to a request from the head of a children's cancer organization located in West Virginia, USA. He explained the troubles he had as a child who fought cancer. He also relayed how those same challenges were being faced by every family that has a child with cancer today. Those challenges included poor nutrition, a lack of culinary understanding, and people simply giving up and letting their kids eat whatever they wanted because they did not understand how to compensate for the changes their children were going through. As a result, this book will challenge you to change and begin to understand new concepts. This book will challenge you to expand the way you think. It will challenge you to imagine new concepts that may make you uncomfortable and break you out of your comfort zone. The people who were most successful with *Cooking for Chemo ...and After!* were the people who were willing to try the new ideas, like the addition of red wine vinegar to common recipes. In this book, I will also challenge many inaccurate superstitions about food and the health benefits of a few life-style choices.

The biggest challenge many people have with my books is that they are mistaken in the thought that they are cookbooks. This is NOT a cookbook. A cookbook is a book that has lists of recipes, ingredients, and very generic descriptions of how to create an item.

This book, *Cooking for Kids with Cancer*, is a self-help guide that teaches you HOW to cook. I like to think of it as a *How-to-Cook Cookbook*. So, if you simply want lists of recipes to try or a quick fix, please look elsewhere. This book is not for you. You will hate it. But, if you want to learn the why, what, and how of cooking for kids undergoing cancer treatment, then you can find no resource any finer than this one.

This book is written for the benefit of children, but it is written for the parents, guardians, and family of children who are fighting cancer. The primary target is the child's caregiver themselves. As a result, I have kept the text at an adult reading level.

The recipes in this text have been tweaked to be child friendly, with many of them coming from *Cooking for Chemo ...and After!* The purpose of these recipes is to simply give you a starting place to practice your new found cooking techniques and skills. These recipes are not intended to be a regimented diet that you must follow for success. It is, as it has always been, the understanding of the taste, flavor, and perception changes that will have the greatest impact for our little cancer fighters.

That being said, I highly recommend working directly with your dietitian and oncologist to come up with a nutritional program that will work best for you and your child. This book is provided as an informational resource only. It is not to be used or relied on for any diagnostic or treatment purposes. This information should not be used in lieu of traditional cancer treatment. We are simply teaching you how to combat many of the eating related side-effects that cancer treatments can cause on your loved one.

In this book, you will find basic culinary information, helpful techniques, innovative ideas about food, basic meal planning information, basic nutritional concepts, and techniques to combat the most common eating related chemotherapy side-effects. I strongly recommend grabbing a highlighter, a pen, and some post-it notes so that you can write down ideas and concepts for you to reference later. It is with this idea that we have printed the book in the form and type of paper that it is made with. I really want you to get this book dirty in the kitchen. This is a hands-on book. We have made the best efforts to keep the price affordable. This is so that if your current copy gets ruined, you can easily replace the book with little effect to your end of month balance sheet.

It is for this reason as well that there are no pictures in this book. Including pictures and a full color print changed the price point of the book. It made it significantly unobtainable by the average person. We have rectified this by integrating our website, *cookingforchemo.org*, with content from our books. The book is now a piece of the entire puzzle. The website provides dynamic content like pictures, videos, extra recipes, and up to date articles that you can read free of charge at any time.

Before you get started with the rest of the book, you will need to purchase the list of ingredients found in the beginning of Chapter 3. The ingredients will be required in Chapter 1 as you begin to taste these ingredients and begin to learn about their flavor.

One last piece to keep in mind. This is a self-published book. We did not have an entire professional production team and several tens of thousands of dollars to spend on the creation of this book. We made this book because we feel that it will help a lot of people that are going through the most difficult time in their life. We have made every effort to create the best content possible, the best layout possible, and to find all of the mistakes that the text contains. But, there may be a few mistakes here and there. I like to think that this adds to the charm and personality of the book! We are focused on helping people first and foremost.

If you ever have questions, contact us through email or social media. I will do my best to personally respond to all of your questions, especially the more challenging questions that I may not have encountered yet or covered in this book.

I wish your family the greatest success in their fight against cancer. You will always be in our family's prayers.

Chef Ryan Callahan

WHY YOU NEED TO READ THIS BOOK

By picking up this book, you have successfully begun the first step in fighting a winning battle against cancer. As I am writing this, it hasn't even quite been a full year since the release of my first book. But, there is the absolute need for a follow up aimed specifically at kids who are fighting cancer on a daily basis. While the battle of adults with cancer is very similar, there are definitely unique challenges that must be overcome that are specific to kids.

I never pictured myself writing a cookbook specifically focused at this demographic, ever. But with the advice of a childhood cancer fighter, I was convinced that this book is something that absolutely must be written.

One of the unique challenges in this audience is an underdeveloped palate or sense of taste. Kids just like different things than adults do. I know that when I was a kid, I was a bit of an odd ball. I actually thoroughly enjoyed foods like broccoli and Brussels sprouts. But most kids do not. This of course presents a unique challenge for me. That challenge is not just to teach you how to adjust your cooking for these tiny cancer fighters but also how to include all of the necessary nutrients that their bodies need to grow and heal.

Another thing to keep in mind is that kids like the foods that you have already exposed them to. My nephews will eat sour and spicy flavors because they have been repeatedly exposed to those flavors. To put this a little more plainly, if all your child has ever been exposed to is things like cheeseburgers, pizza, and sugary cereals, it will come as a complete and total shock to them when all of a sudden their plate is filled with fresh foods like mushrooms, zucchini, chickpeas, lentils, and tofu. So you need to take into consideration what they have been exposed to previously and what their current diet looks like. Think of it like a goldfish. When you get a goldfish back from the store, it comes in a little bag. You don't simply drop the goldfish into the bowl and say, "good luck goldfish." You slowly incorporate water from the fish's new bowl into its bag so that it can learn to adjust to the new water it now lives in. The same is true for kids. If you raised your child on a vegetarian diet, you can't throw a piece of prime rib on their plate and simply tell them to eat it. Their body doesn't know what to do with it. Your child will end up being sicker than a dog. So, we need to incorporate changes to the diet in slow incremental steps.

A little known fact about the world. We as human beings are nothing more than the sum of our parts. Which is to say, we are nothing more than what people have created us to be. We are nothing more than a sum of our life experiences, if you will. And nowhere is that more prevalent and more visible than in young people who are fighting cancer. Often, kids will dislike a food or flavor. It's not because they inherently do not like something. It's because they simply have not been exposed to that food or flavor often enough to understand it. But, there are a few specific flavors that every person likes irregardless of age or experience. Those are the 3 flavors of salty, savory, and sweet.

Sweet is probably the easiest for a person to understand because what do we give our kids as treats or rewards? We give them sugar. The kids ingest the sugar which lights up the pleasure centers of the brain releasing happy thoughts and feelings. Now whatever behavior they were doing to get the treats is reinforced. This book is full of helpful information like this. I do fully intend on challenging your preconceived notions, hearsay, and over turning any false information that has been fed to you about food and nutrition. Let me tell you. The cancer world is full of lies, deception, and false information disseminated by well meaning charlatans with their own political agendas. But with this book, we will cut through it all. I will teach you the life changing culinary information that will help you and your family get through this tough time.

Tommy's Story

One of the reasons I am so passionate about this subject is because my best friend, Tommy, died from cancer as a young adult. He was part of the inspiration for my first book, *Cooking for Chemo ...and After!* And he is the reason that I am writing this book today. So that no one else has to go through what I went though, which was watching by best friend wither away until his ultimate death.

Before we get bogged down into too much information, I feel it is appropriate to tell Tommy's story so that you can understand what we are fighting for. This is something that I don't like to talk about. It makes me feel extremely guilty and sad. September 1st 2008 is the day that my best friend Tommy breathed his last breath and died. He died at home in his sleep. He was surrounded by his family. He lost his battle to stage 4 liver cancer that had metastasized into his lungs. His parents had emigrated from Vietnam to start a new life and to offer a better life to their children.

Tommy was by all accounts the nicest, kindest, and most charitable person that anyone had ever met. He dropped out of high school to focus on his one true passion which was his love for martial arts. One week before Tommy died, he was awarded a 4th degree black belt in Tae Kwon Do by his teacher, Master Park. The significance of this is that Tommy's life long dream had been to open his own dojo and pass on his love for the sport to the next generation. To be considered a true master, you had to have a 4th degree black belt. In this goal, he worked tirelessly to eat healthy, work out constantly, and by any account he was a model for fitness and physical health.

Tommy was actually diagnosed with cancer after returning from a martial arts tournament in Korea, where he gave an Olympic medalist in Tae Kwon Do a solid run for their money. After beginning aggressive chemotherapy treatments, Tommy found it almost impossible to taste or eat any food except for a couple of select junk foods which were the only things he could taste.

Tommy was diagnosed the last week of July 2008 and by September 1st he was gone. In the process, he had wasted away down to nothing. So how did this happen? How did a 21 year old kid, in the peak of physical health, get cancer and then subsequently die from it? What so many people would tell you is the absolute contrary. There are charlatans in the world who will tell you that diet and exercise alone will cure all cancers. And here is the evidence that this is simply not true.

What caused Tommy's death was a very common complication from an aggressive chemotherapy regimen: malnutrition leading to starvation. This is a subject that is very rarely, if ever, discussed. But any oncologist, if they are willing, can tell you they have seen it. It unfortunately happens more frequently than you would think. There are many eating related side-effects to chemotherapy treatments such as mouth sores, nausea, loss of appetite, and metallic tastes to name a few. Understanding how to combat these is the key in doing everything you can to prevent what happened to Tommy from happening to your child and other young adults.

So let's discuss Tommy a little bit further. After his chemotherapy began, the only two things that agreed with him where salty, savory snacks and cookies. As you can imagine, this is not exactly the best recipe for good health. This is why learning how to compensate for flavor changes during cancer treatment is so important. Because everything tasted metallic to Tommy, he wouldn't eat any of the nutritious meals that his family and friends tried to make for him. If they had understood that there are a few simple cooking tricks and techniques, like Palate Cleansing and Roundness of Flavor to combat these eating related side-effects, they could have helped him eat. But eventually, they just gave up and let him eat whatever he wanted. They simply didn't know what else they could do.

What they didn't know was the concept of pungency. When you go through chemotherapy treatments, your nose becomes extremely sensitive to certain smells. Vietnamese cooking uses an extremely delicious but very pungent sauce called fish sauce. If you've ever been to a Vietnamese restaurant, it's that strangely stinky but very delicious sauce that everything gets tossed in. This pungent sauce, while extremely delicious, should never be used when cooking for people going through chemotherapy because the pungency of the sauce may induce nausea. As a result, it can cause a loss of appetite. Even in those who grew up with it, like Tommy.

Another thing that would have really helped Tommy, would have been the understanding of Roundness of Flavor. Roundness of Flavor is my cooking theory that all of your body senses are interlinked during the eating process. You don't simply experience food with your mouth, but with all of your senses at the same time. During cancer treatment, your senses come out of alignment and your sense of smell can become more sensitive. Foods that you used to love can now taste horrible. The tongue actually only perceives 5 flavors: salty, savory, spicy, sour, and sweet. All of the other flavors that you experience actually come from your sense of smell. And while I don't necessarily believe that your nose gets super powers from chemotherapy, I do believe that you become more aware of your noses ability to perceive danger from your foods. One of you noses primary functions is actually as a danger sniffer. Kind of like how we use dogs to sniff out bombs and drugs at airports. Your nose does the exact same thing. Ever smell expired milk? You take a big ole whiff and your body's physiological reaction is to regurgitate the contents of your stomach. This is a defense mechanism. Your nose detected danger and it hits the panic switch to keep you from getting food poisoning. During chemotherapy, this panic switch can be on a hair tight trigger. This can cause all kinds of foods that never made you sick previously to now cause nausea. It is the knowledge of these things happening that allows us to make better decisions in our cooking and our eating and to avoid these smells entirely.

One of the other debilitating side-effects that chemotherapy causes is a persistent metallic taste in your mouth. We can combat this with a cooking technique I refer to as Palate Cleansing. Palate Cleansing both removes metallic taste from food and removes the perceived weight of a dish simultaneously. This allows us to get more nutrient dense meals into our loved one than if we had not used this technique at all. The technique is incredibly simple. You can achieve this cooking technique by simply adding 1-2 tablespoons of red wine vinegar and a proportional amount of sugar to your meal in the middle of cooking. The vinegar will help to lighten the weight of the dish and to help combat the metallic taste by leaving a clean feeling in your mouth at the end of the bite. Vinegar also helps remove pungency from your food and will also help to make your food feel less heavy and greasy in your mouth. The sugar in this Palate Cleansing technique masks the taste and smell of the vinegar which allows it to work its' magic without creating an offensive odor or taste in your food.

In Tommy's ability to only eat junk food, we can learn a little insight into what his body was actually craving. The craving for salty and savory tells us that his body was craving but not receiving protein. And in the craving and eating of the sugary sweet cookies, it was going after the basic carbohydrates that fuel your body to keep you going everyday. Tommy had an incredibly low body fat percentage which gave his body almost no energy reserves. As a result, he began wasting away as soon as he stopped being able to eat. If we take the time to understand what these cravings are and then how to season our food in a way that compensates for these cravings, we can begin to cook nutritious meals that will satisfy those cravings and allow our loved one to enjoy what they are eating.

The last thing you need to understand is what flavors you need to properly season your food. I will also be teaching this technique to you in this book. We season our foods by focusing on the tongue first. We season our meals by using these flavors, in this order, in small increments. The order of these flavors are: salty, savory, spicy, sour, sweet. Next, we add aromatic herbs and spices to our meals to both overcome pungency and to help make our meals more appetizing.

The reason I recommend seasoning in this order is because salt amplifies the natural flavors of the food. Savory tells your body that this food is nutritious. Spicy again amplifies the flavors and adds a fulfilling warmth to your food. Sour lightens and refines the flavors in your food. And sweet tells your body this is full of energy, balances the sour flavor, and rounds out the flavor of the entire meal. Hence why this idea is called, Roundness of Flavor. We will discuss these ideas in greater detail in Chapters 1 and 2.

While what happened to Tommy was most certainly a tragedy, I believe that his early demise could have been prevented or at the very least, prolonged, if I had understood and had been able to teach these cooking techniques to him and his family when he started his short but harrowing with fight with cancer. It is my wish to pass these cooking techniques and ideas onto you and your family so that you don't befall the same fate.

CHAPTER 1:
UNDERSTANDING FLAVOR

Calling someone a bad cook or a good cook is a misnomer. There truly is only one difference between a good cook and a bad cook. That difference is experience. If you believe yourself to be a bad cook, I want you to throw all of those thoughts out of your head right now. There is no such thing as a bad cook. You are simply an inexperienced cook. But I assure you with some practice, a positive attitude, and this book, you will learn how to cook like an experienced chef in no time. Understanding flavor is incredibly important when cooking for kids with cancer. So, I invite you to make the effort because our loved ones are worth it.

In this chapter, I am going to teach you about my personal theory: "Roundness of Flavor—" what it is, how to create it, and how all of your senses come into play when cooking. You will also learn fundamentals of flavor— what primary, secondary, complimentary, and contradictory flavor senses are and how to use them. Let's begin.

What is Roundness of Flavor?

Roundness of Flavor is best described as a holistic view of the entire eating and tasting sensory experience. Now, when I say holistic, I do not intend to use it in the modern sense of the word which generally refers to vegetarianism, organic process, or alternate medicines. I mean holistic in the actual sense of the word, which is to take all factors and treat them as a whole. High quality cooking encompasses all of your senses: taste, smell, touch, sight, and sound. When you eat, you perceive food with not just one sense but with all five senses. You see the food. You hear the sound that the food makes. You smell the food on your plate. You feel the temperature and texture of the food in your mouth and on your lips. And you taste the food when it is inside your mouth. Each sense lends itself to the complete sensory experience. So now, let's explore each sense individually.

Taste

Taste itself, is in reality only a small fraction of the sensory experience. What you actually taste when you eat are 5 primal flavors which are: salty, savory, spicy, sour, and sweet. Each one of these basic taste sensations lends itself as a piece of the whole sensory experience. What chemotherapy does, is it leads to the diminishment of the ability to perceive these flavors. You have to remember that chemotherapy is more like an atomic bomb than a surgical strike. It effects every aspect of every system in your body. So why wouldn't it naturally effect taste? Beyond diminishment of your sense of taste, chemotherapy's main taste side-effect is an ever present taste of metal in your mouth. The best thing we can do is to find out which of our 5 primal taste senses has come out of balance and adjust for them in our cooking. For example, I found that my mom preferred to eat foods that were a little extra sweet and a little extra savory. By adjusting your seasonings for these flavor changes, you can easily overcome these side-effects.

Smell

Any flavor you experience beyond the above described basic taste senses, is your sense of smell. Because your sense of smell has the ability to differentiate over trillions of individual unique scents, you can build much richer sensory experiences through smell than you could ever build through taste. But because your sense of smell and your sense of taste are so interlinked, that unless we stop and separate the two, we would never naturally notice their interdependence. Smell is in fact such a powerful sense that when you think of memories in your mind, you can actually remember the smell that the event had. Think about your grandfathers cologne or the way Thanksgiving dinner smells. If you really close your eyes and concentrate, you will notice that as you think of these memories, you can actually re-smell the events in your mind as if they were happening right now. We want to use this sense of smell to our advantage when cooking for someone going through chemotherapy.

For example, let us pretend that you have a pot roast simmering in a slow cooker. Your house is filled with the smell of pot roast. As a result, it smells so good you can taste it, right? Wrong. You don't actually taste the pot roast just from smelling it. But, you are using your sense of smell to experience the flavor for you. The most complicated flavors that you will experience are generated not by your tongue's interaction with your food but with your nose's interaction with your food.

Another thing you absolutely must know is the concept of pungency. Pungency is simply defined as how powerful the smell of an item is. For example, roses have a light smell and are not very pungent. But, old fish is very pungent and will have an off-putting smell. Some would say that smell is stinky. To differentiate, pungency describes the quantity of smell. Where as stinky describes the quality of smell. Understanding the variations in the strength of pungency is something you will learn to develop as time goes on and as you become more proficient with your cooking techniques.

Since chemotherapy patients can have a heightened sense of smell for some food items, but a diminished sense of smell for other items. It is extremely important to be able to distinguish between the smell of foods that will make your loved one hungry and the foods that will put them off completely. It is best to avoid overly pungent foods and spices when cooking and flavoring. I recommend keeping a tasting journal where you write down your loved one's reactions to each meal. I have created *Chef Ryan Callahan's Tasting Journal* which you can use for ease and convenience to track these changes.

The best example of pungency, that I can think of, occurred while my mother was going through chemotherapy treatments for breast cancer. My mom loves canned tuna. But during chemotherapy, she would become nauseous as soon as she'd crack a can open. This nausea would also occur if I would open a can of tuna for myself on the completely opposite side of the house. The pungent scent would travel down the hall and still cause her to be nauseous from a distance. This example illustrates the power of the nose and it's control over your body. Remember to be conscious of what you eat when your loved one is going through cancer treatments, it can affect them negatively.

Touch

Beyond taste and smell, another major player during cancer treatments is your tactile sense, or sense of touch. This factor comes into play in the guise of heat sensitivity, mouth dryness, and mouth sores. These are all unfortunate but common side-effects of the cancer treatment experience. Taking these side-effects into account is extremely important as their pain and discomfort can completely over power the pleasure had from the eating experience. This can of course lead to dehydration, malnutrition, and starvation. So, we must compensate for these effects when we think of a dish or meal as a whole.

Another form, that sense of touch takes while eating is a concept that I refer to as the weight of a dish. Weight is the perception of thickness, density, viscousness, or actual physical heaviness from your food in your mouth. When cancer patients eat food, the taste and smell are diminished as a chemotherapy side-effect. The major sensation you are left with is your sense of touch, which you may not be used to experiencing in full consciousness. As a result, soft but heavy textures like oatmeal, shepherd's pie, or pot roast may feel suspiciously heavy in your mouth. As a result, the weight can make them unappetizing. When you combine this with the sensitivity caused by mouth sores, you end up with a recipe for disaster.

Sight

Sight is definitely an important part of cooking for kids going through cancer treatments. We want to prepare our food to be not only healthy and filling but look appetizing too. Sight is an important factor because it is the only other sense besides smell that will make you disinterested in a meal from a distance. The sight of food can even go so far as to make you nauseous and loose your appetite. One of the things that I did for my mom while she went through chemotherapy was to make certain that every dish I made had a variety of brightly colored and fresh, but cooked, vegetables inside the dish whenever possible. Brightly colored vegetables in your meals preload your brain with the idea that what you are about to eat is fresh, light, and healthy.

Sound

Sound comes into play with cooking in a variety of ways. The main way sound comes into play is through a theory called classical conditioning. This is where a researcher named Pavlov discovered that he could make his dog hungry and salivate simply by ringing a bell. To make a long story short, every time Pavlov went to feed his dog, he would ring a bell. He did this for so long that the dog began to associate the sound of the bell with food. As such, Pavlov could simply ring the bell and make his dog hungry. Pavlov's bell ringing doesn't make a very good super power. But, we can use the concept of association on our loved ones to trick their brain into making them hungry.

One of the ways we can do this is by using that same theory of association whenever we prepare a meal. When I was my mothers caregiver, any time I would make food for her, I would always begin by sautéing garlic. The sound and the smell of the garlic sautéing over time, slowly programmed my mom's brain into preparing her to eat.

This same idea can be applied in any fashion, whether it is sautéing garlic or ringing a bell. If we can train the brain to associate a sound with eating, just like Pavlov's dogs, our loved ones will begin to drool a little too—in a good way!

Some other examples of this would be when you hear Italian music in an Italian restaurant. It puts you in the mood to eat some really good Italian food. Also, the sound and smell of frying bacon makes you salivate and your tummy rumble as you prepare it for breakfast. These sounds mentally prepare you and tell your stomach to be excited about eating food. We must learn to use this to our advantage.

Now that we have an overview of all of the senses and how they interplay with the eating experience, we can now begin to build an understanding of flavor, what it is, and how it works.

Flavor Basics

Flavor is a tricky and complicated concept. It is made up of many different aspects of senses as well as senses in their entirety. Let's start with the basics of the tongue. The human tongue only tastes a few basic flavors. This is actually such a controversial subject that it is still hotly debated whether or not certain flavors constitute tasting or just a secondary experience. The most commonly accepted flavors that your tongue tastes are: salty, savory, sour, bitter, and sweet. I like to add spicy to this list as well, seeing as you experience spicy on your tongue just like the other flavors. The seasoning methods to combat sour and bitter are almost identical, so for simplicity—and for our sanity—we will say that the following are the flavors that you actually taste with your tongue: salty, savory, spicy, sour, and sweet.

So, let's have some fun at home and learn what role your tongue plays in developing flavor. We're going to do an experiment tasting different seasonings and truly experiencing them for the first time.

Chef Ryan's Sensory Perception Test

Ingredients Needed

kosher salt
soy sauce
MSG
red pepper or cayenne pepper
vinegar
lemon or lime juice
sugar

Directions

First, wash and dry your hands to avoid cross-contamination. In a series of small containers, place each of the above ingredients. Make certain none of them are touching or contaminated. Before you taste each one, pinch your nose to stop the sensation of smell from becoming involved. This is so that you can finally taste something purely with your tongue and not with your sense of smell. Now, with the tip of your finger, taste each one individually. Wash your mouth out and finger off with water before trying the next ingredient. Using the basic senses we just described, write down what each one tasted like to you.

Ingredient	Taste of Ingredient
kosher salt	salty
soy sauce	salty and savory
MSG	savory - If it tastes like nothing, add a little salt. MSG is activated by the presence of salt.
red pepper or cayenne pepper	spicy
red wine vinegar	sour
lemon or lime	sour and sweet at the same time
sugar	sweet

Did you notice how the flavors that you associate with each item vary greatly from what you think of in your mind verses what the actual flavor is inside of your mouth? Since salt mostly activates in the front portion of your tongue, those are the taste receptors that come alive when you taste it. Savory perception is mostly located in the back of your tongue. It often feels like a very subtle and muted flavor. Knowing where the location of each flavor sense exists isn't the important part of this lesson. It is in knowing that your tongue has dedicated flavor receptors for each flavor and that they are not mixed in together evenly. This should be your first ah-ha moment of this book. You have just begun to discover how each part of your body comes into play when you perceive flavor.

Now, let's do this experiment again. But this time, describe how your mouth physically feels after each item.

Ingredient	How It FEELS In Your Mouth
kosher salt	dry
soy sauce	dry and coated
MSG	lightly coated
red pepper or cayenne pepper	sensation of physical heat in your mouth
red wine vinegar	clean
lemon or lime	clean and crisp
sugar	sticky

So why does the way food feels in your mouth matter? The reason you need to know how something feels in your mouth when cooking for cancer and chemotherapy patients is because getting food into them has a lot to do with the weight of the dish. "Weight" is the sensation of food in your mouth. A dish's weight can be any where from heavy to light just like all physical objects. The difference is that excess weight in your meals can make eating extra difficult when you are going through cancer treatments.

For example, a pot roast tends to be very heavy in weight. It is filled with proteins, starches, and fats. It generally causes a heavy feeling in your stomach and in your mouth during and after eating. This would be an example of a heavily weighted dish. On the other hand a nice Greek salad, with vinaigrette dressing and the whole nine yards of fresh ingredients in it, is a lightly weighted dish. The large amount of calories from complex animal fats is one of the many reasons the pot roast feels heavier in weight than the Greek salad. The other aspect that makes the pot roast feel heavier is the lack of acidity in the meal. By utilizing a few tablespoons of red wine vinegar, we can change the dish from feeling heavy in your mouth to feeling lighter in weight. This will make it more satisfying as you eat it. For a chemotherapy patient, this light and crisp finish in your meal is the difference between getting a whole bowl's worth of high-impact nutrients into their body or simply a few spoonfuls.

The biggest reason we need to be aware of food weight is so we can learn how to trick your brain into allowing you to eat more food during chemotherapy. We learn how to do to this in the up-coming sections with a technique I call Palate Cleansing.

Balancing Flavor

When a chef cooks, what he is trying to do is bring out the fullness of flavor, or roundness of flavor. This brings us to our next lesson.

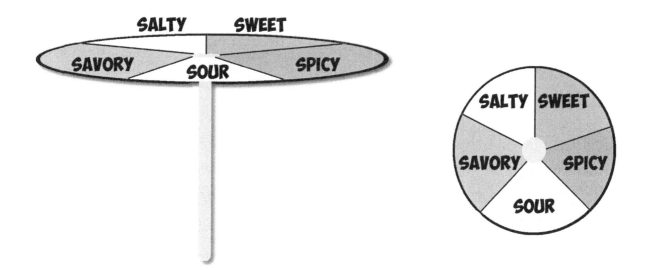

Think about the results of our sensory perception test and what you know these flavors to be. Now take a look at our chart above for a great visual representation of what I call *Roundness of Flavor*.

Imagine the circular dish above is mounted on a thin piece of metal so that it acts as a scale. As you apply weight to any category, like salty, the dish will tip toward the salty side. As you place each flavor on the dish, it will lean from side to side, eventually balancing out. What you want to do is weigh out the proper amounts of flavor onto this imaginary dish so that the dish doesn't topple over and become one-sided.

Cooking is about balance, harmony, and pulling the natural flavors out of your ingredients. All food items that you eat have their own natural flavors and will pre-stack the weight of the dish. As we add items to our meals, we need to be conscious of their natural flavors and how they will make the dish balance.

This lesson is the single most important part of this book. It is the lesson we will be coming back to over and over. Finding Roundness of Flavor is the key in feeding people going through cancer treatment. Because their senses are all out of alignment, the flavor balance that may taste great to you, might taste terrible to them. When we are *cooking for kids with cancer*, we want to use Roundness of Flavor to realign our senses to compensate for their flavor changes.

I found that those undergoing cancer treatment, especially chemotherapy, prefer to eat foods that are a little extra sweet and a little extra savory. Some people have even told me that all they could eat were spicy foods. And others had to avoid spicy all together.

Roundness of Flavor helps you address your individual needs. It breaks down the puzzle into manageable pieces so that you can put the puzzle back together in a way that individually works best for your loved one going through cancer treatment. Keep a tasting journal to track what flavors your loved one enjoys and the ones that they don't.

Aromatics: The Nose To Our Food

Now that we are familiar with taste and all of our other senses, we need to talk a little more in depth about smell. Or, what I call "the nose to your food." You can make many fantastic dishes with very basic ingredients, like salt, MSG, pepper, vinegar, and sugar. But, what we want to do is give our food some character, maybe add a few aromatic qualities to give our food even more appeal. To do this, we are going to add spices and herbs. Many times people get confused as to what the differences are between the two. It's very simple.

Spices tend to be derived from the roots, bark, flowers, or seeds of a flavorful plant.

Herbs are dried *(or fresh)* leaves of edible plants that impart an aromatic flavor.

To make it easier:

Spices
Cinnamon *(bark)*
Nutmeg *(seed)*
Cloves *(flower)*
Coriander *(seeds)*

Cumin *(seed)*
Ginger *(root)*
Black pepper *(seed)*

Herbs
Oregano *(leaves)*
Basil *(leaves)*
Thyme *(leaves)*
Marjoram *(leaves)*
Lavender *(needles)*
Rosemary *(needles)*
Cilantro *(leafy vegetation of the Coriander plant)*

For your convenience, there is a *Herbs and Spices Chart* at the end of the book.

As you'll learn in your cooking journey, eastern cooking styles favor spices and western styles favor herbs. This simply has to do with the local availability of products as the different cultures and cooking techniques developed. The other difference is that spices tend to be used in conjunction with other spices, like in curry. Whereas herbs tend to be used by themselves, like a sprig of rosemary on lamb.

A fantastic way to remember the difference between herbs and spices is: "Roses are red. Violets are blue. Herbs are green and freshest too!"

I want to take some time to talk about the age of herbs and spices and how it effects the potency of its flavor. Time changes the flavor of everything regardless of whether it is fresh fruit, a fresh steak, or dried foods such as dried spices. With dried herbs and spices, it is really important that 1) they stay dry and 2) they are not too old because they will loose their potency. Just because something is dried or preserved does not mean that it will keep its strength when it comes to flavor. Simply remember to keep in mind that time can not only diminish the flavor but also alter or change the flavor of your foods. Think about yogurt. Yogurt starts as milk. Then bacterial cultures are added. Time passes and changes the flavor, structure, and consistency of the product resulting in something completely different in the end.

Potency of spices is very important to take into consideration because measurements used will vary based on the strength of the spice. Oregano that is five years old is not going to be nearly as strong as oregano that was just recently dried. You will have to use a lot more of the five-year-old oregano to compensate for the loss of flavor. Also, certain spices and herbs will actually change flavor and smell over time. This is especially true for herbs like thyme and sage. They get musty and stinky. Cinnamon is an example of a spice that will lose its potency too. You need to know this because recipes will call for a certain amount of an ingredient. And if your seasonings are stale, the recipe will not turn out right. The flavor profile will end up being completely off.

Many times you will blend both herbs and spices to bring out the flavor of whatever food you are preparing. A great rule of thumb is to remember not to over season but to start out by under seasoning. We always want to under season our food while cooking. We do this because you can always add more seasonings but not necessarily take away. So when you are seasoning a dish, season with about half the amount of seasoning that the recipe calls for. As the dish gets closer to finishing, taste the dish. Then, in small increments, slowly add the additional seasoning that the recipe will require. If you follow this method, you will never end up with a meal that is over-seasoned. This is especially true with the recipes listed in this book. The recommended seasonings in this book are by no means scientifically accurate measurements. Very often, I actually measure by pouring spices or seasonings into my hand. In transcribing these recipes, I may have not converted them properly.

In addition to this, you must keep in mind that no recipe is perfect. Often other cooks use the same method as I use and take wild stabs in the dark at how much seasoning they actually put into a recipe. This isn't to say that other cooks are necessarily being lazy or intentionally inaccurate. It is simply that cooking is an art. Cooking is about building flavors like building a brick wall. We stack the flavors brick by brick until we have a wall. Throwing all the seasonings in at once seems like you would be building that wall faster. But in the end, all you are truly left with is a large heap of bricks.

28

You should also keep in mind that you may become more or less sensitive to different seasonings in different recipes depending on the ingredients in the recipe. This is especially true with spicy. Because spicy flavors can vary in strength from brand to brand and even within the product its self, always add just a little bit of spicy at a time. A great example of this is a container of red pepper that I have. One dash of this red pepper is equivalent to 4 or 5 dashes from other bottles from the same manufacturer. This same fact is true for everything that we eat. This is because no two of the same item are identical. Two Roma tomatoes, even from the same plant, will not be identical in every way. The same is true for humans, dogs, cats, eggplants, and everything else that is or was ever living. This is simply the nature of life in the universe. Because it was living and growing, it is therefore always unique.

The other thing you need to remember when cooking is that you are not trying to change the flavor of the ingredients but compliment what you are already cooking. The goal is to bring out the naturally occurring flavors of the ingredients. This is one of the areas of cooking where Chinese and Italian cooking styles agree: always season to emphasize and celebrate how delicious your ingredients are! A good rule of thumb is if both the Chinese and the Italians are doing it, it must be good! Let's look at an example of seasonings in practice and what they are being used for. Please turn to the next page.

Roasted Chicken with Bouquet Garni

Ingredients
1 family-sized roasting chicken, defrosted

Flavor Balancers
kosher salt (or any course salt)
black pepper, fine ground
1 tbsp. (15 ml) butter

Aromatics
garlic, minced
3 bay leaves
1 sprig rosemary
2 sprigs thyme
1 sprig parsley

Recipe Directions
Place the chicken in a roasting pan. Fill the bottom of the pan with 1 inch *(2 centimeters)* of water. Melt the butter and apply to the outside of the chicken's skin. Generously apply salt, pepper, and garlic. To make your bouquet garni, tie the following herbs together with string to make a bundle: 1 sprig rosemary, 2 sprigs thyme, 1 sprig parsley, and 3 bay leaves. Place the bouquet garni in the water. Cover chicken with aluminum foil making certain to keep the edges tight around the roasting pan. Roast at 350° F *(175° C)* until breast meat reaches an internal temperature of 165° F *(about two to three hours)*. Baste chicken frequently during cooking to make sure all the flavors get mixed thoroughly.

Chef Tips
Remove aluminum tenting during the last 30 minutes of cooking to give the chicken a nice crispy skin. Broth chicken sits in can also be used as gravy or can be filled with veggies before cooking to help soak up all the extra flavor! You can also alternatively place the bouquet garni in the open cavity of the chicken or chop up the herbs and place them on top of the chicken before baking avoiding having the make a bouquet garni at all.

Dissecting The Recipe

In this recipe, we have the following seasonings to consider: rosemary, thyme, parsley, bay leaves, salt, and black pepper. For ease of discussion, we won't consider garlic a seasoning. We will consider it an aromatic ingredient.

Salt serves several functions in this dish: 1) to help tenderize the meat 2) to bond with the glutamate and nucleotides in the meat, creating a more savory flavor 3) to add saltiness to the dish, helping to establish our roundness of flavor and 4) acting as a flavor amplifier to the rest of the dish.

Black pepper acts as an aromatic agent as well as lighting up those spicy receptors!

Rosemary gives the chicken an aromatic and fragrant richness, emboldening the flavors.

Thyme acts as a lighter version of rosemary adding fragrance to the dish.
Parsley helps to lighten the flavor of the dish by adding freshness.

Bay leaves add aromatic richness as well as increasing the savory flavor of the chicken.

So what we end up with is a rich, savory, and fragrant chicken! These flavors, or tastes, are the basic fundamentals of flavor. They are the beginning of the road to not only cooking but cooking like a great chef!

Secondary Flavor Senses

Now as we are trying to build our Roundness of Flavor, it is important to keep in mind one other thing. Sometimes, we are trying to construct a dish that specifically bolsters one flavor element. Two examples of this would be: 1) buffalo style chicken wings and 2) sweet and sour chicken. These are examples of dishes where the end goal would not necessarily be to make the flavors round and equal, but to use the other flavors to compliment the primary flavor of spicy or sweet and sour.

Let's take the example of buffalo style chicken wings and deconstruct the flavor profile of a common recipe. For those of you who aren't familiar with buffalo style chicken wings, they are bone-in chicken wing ends. These are *(preferably)* deep-fried, then covered in a spicy, tangy sauce.

Usually the sauce is made like this: 8 ounces Frank's Red Hot Sauce + 8 ounces melted butter *(2 sticks)*. That gives the wings a creamy, spicy, and tangy sauce.

The questions we need to ask ourselves are: What ingredients give the wings a creamy, spicy, and tangy flavor? And how can we improve on the flavor of a common recipe?

To answer the first question: The hot sauce is primarily constructed of cayenne peppers that have been infused into a vinegar-based solution. Butter tends to have a sweet and savory taste to it. So when you combine hot sauce and butter, you get sweet and savory from the butter, spicy from the chilies, and sour from the vinegar in the sauce.

So in the grand scheme, where does this new tangy flavor come into play? Tangy comes from the application of both sour and sweet taste buds at the same time. What is happening in your mouth is that the sour flavor is telling your brain that this food is dry and astringent which causes your mouth to salivate more. But, the sweet flavor is activating the pleasure centers of your brain filling you with endorphins that tell your brain, "This is great! Eat more!" This is also known as the sweet and sour effect.

The same confusing experience can be demonstrated by grasping two pipes filled with water. If one has cold water and the other warm water, it will confuse the sensory nerves in your hands and tell your brain "Danger! This is Hot!" Even though the pipes are not hot, your brain believes it is in danger and kicks your survival reflexes in to prevent further potential skin damage. In this same way, the application of both sweet and sour taste receptors confuses your brain causing both pleasure and pain.

Tangy is a perfect example of a secondary flavor sense in action. These secondary flavor senses help to create the complex flavors that we experience when we eat everyday foods.

A secondary flavor sense is only considered secondary when two specific flavors are activated. For example, if we added MSG *(savory)* to our sweet and sour sauce, causing the tangy flavor to be overwhelmed, we would no longer consider it a secondary flavor but a blended, complimentary flavor.

To answer the second question: One of the things we can do to improve this chicken wing recipe is we can start by adding salt. When salt is added to savory flavors, it generates a secondary flavor sense I call *amplified savory.*

The single most important concept in seasoning is that both salty and spicy are flavor amplifiers. What this means is that anything you add salt or spiciness to is going to amplify the flavors of the food already present. Unless you add them in such amounts that they overwhelm the already existing flavors to become the dominant flavors of the dish. Interestingly, the only two flavors that are commonly eaten in western cooking without other complimentary flavors are sweet and savory. Think of hard candies or a big hunk of meat right off the grill. These items are still generally improved with the addition of a little salt, but can very commonly be eaten without.

What else could we add to chicken wings to improve them? We could add black pepper for aromatics and a different type of spicy. *(Yes, each source of spiciness delivers spicy in a different way.)* We could also add garlic for warmth and aromatic quality. And, we can add a touch of sugar for a more balanced tangy flavor.

Most people don't notice secondary flavors because in most dishes they blend in with the other ingredients to fill the whole of flavor perception becoming complimentary flavors.

Some more examples of secondary flavors would be salty and sweet candy *(Juxtaposed Sweet)*, sweet and sour sauce *(tangy)*, pickle brine before it has had anything but salt and vinegar added *(amplified sour)*, and soy sauce *(amplified savory)*.

To help make it easier for you to understand, here is a breakdown of secondary flavors.

Secondary Flavor Senses Chart

Combined Flavors	Resulting Secondary Flavor
Salty + Savory	Amplified Savory
Sweet + Sour	Tangy
Salty + Sour	Amplified Sour
Salty + Sweet	Juxtaposed Sweet
Spicy + Sweet	Heated Sweet

Complimentary and Contradictory Flavors

Flavor works a lot like colors on a color wheel. Some flavors are bright and bold. Some flavors are muted and subtle. But each flavor works together with the other flavors and senses to build a color of each food. Just as an artist picks colors to paint on canvas, we will pick flavors to paint onto our foods.

Complimentary flavors are flavors that blend together so well that they blend into one single continuous flavor, like amplified savory. Contradictory flavors are flavors that seem like they shouldn't go together, but for some reason they bring out new aspects of each flavor *(like tangy and juxtaposed sweet)*.

For a moment, let's pretend we've mixed all of the colors together in a bucket. Depending on the amount of black in the paint, you'll usually end up with some form of brown. What we are trying to do is to blend all the colors, or in this case flavors, until we get some kind of brown. Now, each dish should be its own form of brown and should exemplify the main ingredients.

For example, beef stew should be more savory. Red curries should be spicy and fragrant. Desserts should be sweet. And potato chips should be salty. This isn't a fact that will change with anything you cook. Just to clarify, when I say we are trying to achieve a "brown," I do not mean that every food should literally be the color brown. What I intend to express is that the flavors of each dish should be well mixed together.

When we cook for kids going through cancer treatment, we are not usually trying to emphasize contrary, or secondary flavors. What we are trying to achieve is to make a nice complimentary flavor! The reason for this is contradictory flavors are dynamic. Dynamic flavors can be overwhelming for someone who has had their flavor palate realigned. But the information I have provided allows you to be a better cook by getting a wider and larger picture of the grand scheme of flavor when cooking.

As you can see, understanding flavor is not difficult but it is fairly complicated. Always remember when you are cooking to take all of your senses into account, not just your sense of taste. In the upcoming chapter, I am going to take these basic concepts and elaborate on them more. I am going to teach you how to use the information that you just learned to help combat the most common chemotherapy and cancer treatment related side-effects.

CHAPTER 2: HOW TO COMBAT COMMON EATING RELATED SIDE-EFFECTS

In the previous chapter, we have talked about practical information that you need to know to feel confident in the kitchen. These are of course our basic building blocks of flavor and what senses go into eating and tasting. Now, we are going to take a more hands on approach. I am going to teach you how to combat the most common eating related side-effects from cancer treatment. These lessons all build on each other. So, even if they are not immediately applicable to your situation, please read all of these so that you are fully equipped to handle anything that comes your way.

How To Combat Metallic Taste

To properly combat metallic taste, I must first teach you how to apply and use my *Roundness of Flavor* technique and teach you about *Palate Cleansing.*

To be blunt, there is simply no way to teach someone to cook without physically doing it. You can learn many other disciplines simply by reading about it. But, cooking is both art and science. Just like you can never truly create great works of art simply by looking at Vincent Van Gogh's paintings. You will never develop the physical techniques of the intricacies inherent inside of the brush strokes to capture the delicateness of color. Such is the same with great food. Learning how to cook is exactly like this. You must try and fail and try and fail until you learn how things work and why. Just like the yoga master refers to the art of yoga as "my practice," so must we take this same approach toward cooking. It is an art that you will continually become greater at every day, every week, and every year. You will learn and grow just like a tree until your roots run so far into the ground that you are an immovable object with years of strength and experience to pull from. So it is with this mind-set, we will approach the next few tasks so that we may practice and learn.

First, I need to explain that I developed these cooking techniques when I was my mothers primary caregiver during her breast cancer treatment. As she went through chemotherapy, the side-effects became progressively worse. Through trial and error, I developed a process that I would follow to create Roundness of Flavor.

Then, I would adjust or "tilt" the dish depending on the flavors and weight that would entice my mom to eat. So I am going to pass these techniques on to you to help you become a more effective cancer fighter.

Below is the method I follow. This is actually the creating flavor part of Roundness of Flavor. When I season dishes, I always season them in the following order:

1) salty
2) savory
3) spicy
4) sour
5) sweet

Salty

Salty is the most basic flavor. It is also the most powerful. It amplifies all other flavors. We start with salty to bring out the naturally occurring flavors in the dish. If we did this flavor later, it could over power the rest of the dish. Adding salt late in the cooking process, could make the flavors too aggressive. Salt also acts as a natural tenderizer. It works its way into meat giving it a massive boost of flavor. Food without salt of any kind is extremely bland. If you can not have salt because of sodium, consider using a salt substitute. Salt is also one of the flavors that you cannot correct if you add too much. If you place too much salt in a dish, it is simply ruined and you have to start over.

Examples of salty items: kosher salt, sea salt, soy sauce, and hard cheeses, like Parmesan.

Savory

I always season savory second because it is the least pronounced of all the flavors. But, it is the most important. The reason it is so important is because it gives you that sense of healthiness and nutrition that comes from a home-cooked meal. Savory is the fullness of taste. It is the sense of warmth that you get when eating a protein filled item. Savory is actually activated by the presence of salty flavor. This is the reason why a steak without salt is extremely bland. But if you add a light pinch of salt, it makes the steak taste like a flavor explosion. There are many ways to create a savory flavor. Whether it is simply adding savory ingredients or using heat to brown your meats and vegetables. Browning these items makes them more savory naturally.

Examples of savory items: soy sauce, MSG, anchovies, green tea, mushrooms, tomatoes, and red wine.

Spicy

Spicy comes third because it is our second amplifying flavor. It is the ingredient that fills our warmth portion of the dish. I also season with spicy third because it is the easiest to counter act by adding more vinegar to balance out the spicy. Please remember that just because you are adding a touch of spicy to a dish does not mean that the dish will necessarily be spicy. Great cooking always encompasses a bit of an imperceptible spicy note that just adds a fuller body. So never feel guilty adding a little bit of spicy to your dishes, especially in amounts that a person cannot detect. To add ingredients that a person cannot name or quite put their finger on is the hallmark of a great chef.

When Cooking for Kids with Cancer though, we want to keep spicy flavors to a minimum. Children tend to be much less spicy tolerant. Using ground black pepper in your dishes is probably sufficient to add that imperceptible spicy note. The exception to this rule would be if your kids have been previously exposed to spicy flavors. Some adult chemotherapy patients report having great success with spicy flavors because it was all they could taste. Everyone is different. Make decisions based on personal preferences and life experiences.

Examples of spicy items: black pepper, cayenne pepper, red pepper flakes, chilies, and many more.

Sour

Sour comes fourth because it is the lightener. Everything we have put into our dishes so far has added breadth, fullness, and warmth. Now, we add complexity. Sour brings freshness that you cannot get through any other means. It removes the physical weight of a dish, similar to how moon boots remove the feeling of weight from your body!

Sour is an amazing flavor that is far underutilized. It can make you feel as if you were eating the freshest, lightest fruit salad in the world. But when applied too heavily and too liberally, it can make your mouth pucker and eyes water. With a masterful hand, sour can be applied in just the right amounts to give heavy dishes a light feeling in your mouth. It can also remove the spiciness while amplifying the flavor of chilies. And, it can cleanse the palate and bring delight to any person who wields it. In my opinion, mastery of sour is another hallmark of a great chef.

I get tons of feedback all the time from people who are terrified of vinegar for no justifiable reason. They simply cannot wrap their mind around the idea of what vinegar is and how it works. You cannot successfully achieve Roundness of Flavor without using a sour flavor in your dishes. You must use ingredients like red wine vinegar in your heavier dishes or else they will simply be too heavy to eat for someone going through cancer treatments. So please, over come your irrational fears and trust me. I really know what I am talking about here. Don't be obstinate. You are reading this book to learn and try something new. So, just do it!

Examples of sour items: red vinegar, red wine vinegar, apple cider vinegar, balsamic vinegar, rice wine vinegar, orange juice, lime juice, lemon juice, and pickle brine.

Sweet

Sweet comes last because it is the great balancer. Sweet activates the pleasure centers of your brain and gets you really excited about eating whatever it is you are eating. Sweet can cover many mistakes when cooking and should be used last because it creates our final piece of complex flavoring.

Chinese cooks have a saying that sugar always follows vinegar. This is because sour needs a balancer just like the idea of yin and yang. When yin gets out of control, it needs yang to balance. The philosophy is all about finding the balance between the two. The same is true for fire and water. Fire keeps water in check by boiling it. And water keeps fire in check by keeping it from getting too hot and consuming everything around it. If you have too much fire, everything gets burned. If you have too much water, the passion and the drive is drowned out. The same is true for sour and sweet. You must keep the two in balance at all times. Sweet also allows you to remove or cover the acidity of a dish. Hence, why most people will add a healthy pour of sugar to their marinara sauce.

Sweet is another place where I get a lot of irrational feedback. I am not telling you to pour a pound of sugar into your meals or eat nothing but refined sugars. What I am explaining to you here is that sweetness balances out the dish. It is one of your 5 fundamental flavors. And, it must be mastered and utilized in order to properly combat the side-effects of cancer treatment. A lot of people are afraid of sugar because somebody offhandedly said to them once that people need to eat less sugar.

What those people were trying to actually express was that most people ingest too much candy, sweets, junk food, soft drinks, etc. When you take control of your food and cook every meal at home, you are not going to end up eating too much sugar. Simply because the nature of cooking at home does not make it easy to over load yourself on sugars. What over loads you on sugar is eating a pint of ice cream, followed by drinking 2 liters of soda, and eating a handful of hard candies to finish off the meal.

Sugar is actually the basic energy that your body uses to fuel itself. The reason your body is hot is because your body is regularly combusting sugars inside of your cells to regulate your body temperature. When there is too much sugar, your body converts it for long term storage into fat cells which is how your metabolic process works. This is why if you eat too much sugar, you gain weight. If you eat too little sugar, you loose weight. The energy inside of food is measured in calories, which is why all of our food labels are labeled with the amount of calories that are contained with the food. This is so that you can empower yourself to make decisions on how many calories you need to fuel your body. It's not scary. It's science. I will discuss more on calories, sugar, nutrition, and the like in the next section of this book.

Sweet can be sourced from the following: raw granulated sugar, brown sugar, fruit juices, soft drinks, and an innumerable amount of places.

I follow the salty, savory, spicy, sour, sweet method because my experience has taught me that this is how you should season. It takes into account many different theories, styles, and cultures perspectives on cooking. As I stated previously, I have found that cooking is both art and science. It is a beautiful alchemy that encompasses so much of the human spirit, life experience, culture, memories, and the soul; that it is like an art. The simple whiff of your favorite dish can transport you to places and times that you didn't even remember existed. It can pull emotions so deep that you didn't even know you had. This is the art of cooking.

To bring it all around, the reason I season in this method is two fold. Years of experience show me scientifically that this is the right way to season. And, years of artistic endeavor also support this method.

Here are some flavor charts that will help you adjust specific flavors in your dishes. You may want to earmark or post a sticky note on this page. It is a super helpful reference to have on hand while you are cooking.

Basic Flavors Chart: Where to find each flavor in its raw essence

Flavor Order	Where to Find
Salty	kosher salt, table salt, seasoned salt, soy sauce
Savory	MSG, anchovies, kelp, red wine, green tea, soy sauce, bay leaves, meats, mushrooms
Spicy	red pepper, cayenne pepper, black pepper, hot sauce
Sour	red wine vinegar, rice vinegar, red vinegar, fermented foods, pickles
Sweet	sugar, brown sugar, molasses, syrup, fruits, honey

Roundness of Flavor Chart: How to correct flavor in a dish

Problem:	Solution:
Dish is bland/not savory	add salt and MSG
Dish has no heat	add red pepper or cayenne
Dish is too spicy	add red wine vinegar
Dish feels heavy in my mouth	add red wine vinegar for a palate cleanser
Dish is bitter/sour	add sugar *(remember: sugar follows vinegar)*
Dish is too sweet	add red wine vinegar
Dish has no pizzazz/aromatic quality	add more herbs or spices

One last thing, when you are trying to correct a dish, always add seasonings in small increments. You don't want to over-correct the dish and have to start over.

Palate Cleansing

The most effective cooking technique to curb metallic taste is what I call the *Palate Cleanse*. Palate Cleansing is a simple cooking technique where you use acidic sour flavors to create a lightweight feeling in your mouth and on your tongue when you eat food. Palate Cleansing is an easy to apply cooking technique to use on your loved ones with cancer who can only eat a couple spoonfuls of food before becoming exhausted from eating.

Palate Cleansing also helps reduce the metallic taste in your mouth. Palate Cleansing does this by cleaning your taste receptors after every bite and overpowering the metallic taste leaving a clean fresh taste in your mouth when eating.

Now, before you say "Ew gross." You need to know that the end result of your recipe won't taste like a jar of pickles! When the palate cleansing technique is applied correctly, you won't even notice it in your food.

There are a few ingredients that you can incorporate into your cooking that really help with Palate Cleansing.

Palate Cleansing Ingredients Chart

Palate Cleansing Ingredient	How To Use It
red wine vinegar	add in the middle of cooking
lemon juice	add at the end of cooking
lime juice	apply to food before serving
orange juice	add during cooking
basil	add fresh on top of finished meal
parsley (Italian flat leaf)	add fresh on top of finished meal
cilantro (fresh leaves of a coriander plant)	add fresh on top of finished meal

Palate Cleansing is very easy. Simply add 1-2 tablespoons of red wine vinegar and an equal amount of sugar to whatever recipe you are cooking while you are cooking it. The sugar masks the taste and flavor of the vinegar, but still allows the vinegar to work its magic in your recipe. The heat from cooking forces the vinegar flavor to mellow and become less harsh as well. You know you have the right amount of vinegar when the recipe is lighter in weight, but NOT sour or altered in taste and flavor. If your meal tastes sour or altered in flavor, this is an indicator that you added to much vinegar.

For those who are a little more savvy, you will have noticed the connection between

Palate Cleansing and *Roundness of Flavor.* The Roundness of Flavor technique actually incorporates the Palate Cleansing method into your cooking naturally. This is why I am so adamant that you must add red wine vinegar and sugar to your food when cooking.

In addition to vinegar, fresh herbs like Italian flat leaf parsley, basil, and cilantro are great palate cleansers to use in your meals as well. Simply chop them up fresh and add them to the top of your recipe immediately before serving breakfast, lunch, or dinner. You may use these fresh herbs in conjunction with the vinegar-sugar method, with positive results. You want to make sure that you add these delicate herbs immediately before serving. The heat from cooking will destroy their delicate flavors that are lent in the Palate Cleansing experience.

Cilantro is the American word for the fresh leaves of a coriander plant. Some people actually cannot taste cilantro properly. So if your child reports that the cilantro tastes like dirt or soap instead of a fresh crisp lemony flavor, they simply lack the proper olfactory receptors to taste the cilantro. This is perfectly normal. Use the Italian flat leaf parsley or basil instead.

Citrus juice can also be added as a palate cleanser. Simply squeeze the citrus fruit over the dish before serving. Take care not to cook the citrus juice into the recipe or it could lose its effect. This technique is most commonly applied in central American and Caribbean style cooking. For example, it is traditional to squeeze fresh lime over tacos. This citric acid will lighten the weight of any heavy meats that are on the taco. It also provides a fresh fruity flavor to the dish. As an added bonus, fresh lemons and limes are packed full of vitamin C, which prevents scurvy. One can never have enough vitamin C.

As you can see with a few simple tricks, combating metallic taste is a completely manageable side-effect to treat.

Understanding Smell When Cooking and Eating

Now that we have a firm grasp on matters of the tongue, let's discuss the matters of the nose. Something like 90 percent of all experiences that you have with food are actually nasal related. This is super important to know because nausea and loss of appetite can be combated by understanding your sense of smell and how to use aromatic herbs and spices inside of your cooking to make food exciting again. I have pointed out earlier in this book that it is the smell of a pot roast that causes you to salivate. So, we will continue with this idea and venture further in-depth into the world of how to use aromatics and your sense of smell to your advantage.

Before we learn the specific compensating techniques, I need to teach you more about what aromatics are.

Aromatics

Aromatics, as I had shown previously in this book, include but are not limited to herbs and spices. Each individual food item has a smell all to its own. Think of the smell of a grilled steak, oranges, or fresh fish. Each food item has a scent all to its own. We must take this smell into account whenever we are preparing a dish. Remember, our objective in preparing this food is not to change the natural flavors of the food. It is to bring out more natural flavor and emphasize the qualities of our foods.

There is an old saying that goes a bit like this: "When a guest compliments a French chef, he will reply, 'Thank you very much,' as if it was he and his skill that was being complimented. But an Italian chef will reply, 'Do not thank me. Thank the ingredients.'"

The lesson in this is a truly great chef knows that any dish is made or broken on the constitution of the ingredients that he or she uses. So we must always endeavor to choose quality ingredients and let them tell us how best to serve them. With this in mind, we want to always smell our ingredients every time. An example of this would be if we have a piece of fish. We want to smell it every single time. Fish should never smell fishy, ever. The smell of fishiness is actually a byproduct of decay of the fish proteins. Fish should always smell like the ocean. If it does not smell fresh and clean like the ocean, you should never ever eat it.

This same thought process should be applied to all foods. When you have produce, smell it. What does it smell like? Does your broccoli smell like broccoli? Does your cauliflower smell like cauliflower? Your nose is the fastest indicator that something is amiss. If you open a loaf of bread and it magically smells like cheese, maybe just maybe, you shouldn't be eating that bread. Have you ever smelled sour milk? The first way to tell that milk is bad is simply by giving it a big sniff.

Chemotherapy sends the entirety of your body's senses and functions out of alignment. One of the functions that is majorly impacted is your sense of smell.

Your sense of smell is actually your strongest sense. You are able to identify a trillion of independent odors. Whereas your eyes can only perceive about 10 million colors. When most people think of smell, they think of dogs. Dogs are always sniffing everything. This is for a very good reason. Through smell, they are able to detect a great many things: food, water, mates, danger, bombs, and even some forms of cancer.

While dogs embrace smell, humans tend to actively shun their sense of smell. People go so far as to look at other people suspiciously when someone smells something. Yes, I know this from personal experience. There is actually some strong evidence that suggests humans actually put off various odors based on their emotional states. Have you ever heard of someone "stinking of desperation?" As a chef, my sense of smell is my greatest strength. Being able to identify different scents and match them to other complimentary scents is one of the aspects that allows you to become a great chef.

So, why do dogs have it all figured out and humans stick their nose up at the idea of smell? Well, that probably has a bit to do with the desire to feel "civilized" and detached from our idea of nature. But that is neither here nor there. What I am going to do is teach you how to regain control of that ever so powerful sense. You will learn to use it to modify your cooking to compensate for cancer and chemotherapy's ravages on your child.

The power of your nose can never be understated. It helps you find food. It tells you when to be hungry. It's a defense mechanism. And it protects you from potential harm.

The very first thing I want you to do is start smelling EVERYTHING!

I want you to smell everything. I want you to smell herbs, spices, vinegar, meat, shoes, newspapers, books, computers, vegetables, clean laundry, dirty laundry, and anything else you can get your hands on. I assure you that people will eyeball you very suspiciously. I have a habit of smelling everything. I smell my flatware when I'm out to eat. I smell my food when other people have cooked it for me. I smell newspapers. I smell my pants and even my shoes before I put them on.

The reason I do this is to find out more information about the item that I am smelling. Smelling flatware at a restaurant tells me a few things. If it smells like chlorine, I know that they use bleach as their sanitizer and that the flatware has recently been washed. If it smells like food, I know that it hasn't been washed and that I should get a different fork.

Smelling food tells me many things about it as well. I can tell the doneness of food by scent. If it is a steak, I can tell if the fat has been cooked long enough to become liquid and move through the meat. I can tell if raw food is past its prime thanks to a signature bacterial odor. I can also tell the pungency and strength of spices so I know how much to use when I am cooking. If I smell my pants, I can tell if they are dirty and if I need to wash them. As you can see, there are a great many uses for smell, both offensive and defensive.

What you want to keep in mind is that while your olfactory sense can be your greatest strength in cooking for your child that is going through chemotherapy, it can also be your greatest enemy.

If your child has cancer, especially if they are going through chemotherapy treatment and are experiencing a loss of appetite or increased nausea, I would strongly advise smelling many different scents and documenting what scents they find appealing, and what scents they find nauseating or sickening. You can do this by keeping track of these smells in a tasting journal. By documenting the positive and the negative smells, this will help build a basic road map that will give you a measurable guide on what to use and what to avoid when you are cooking.

Let me ask a simple question. What is the purpose of aromatics in food? The simple answer is: The aroma or aromatic quality of food in each dish is the defining quality and character that separates it from the other dishes.

Let's use the following foods as an example.
moo shu chicken
shredded chicken tacos
chicken shawarma sandwich

These 3 meals are all fundamentally very similar. Ultimately, there is a starchy bread-like substance that acts like a wrapper, a crunchy vegetable aspect, and a soft but flavorful protein aspect to each one of these dishes. On paper, these dishes look extremely similar. But as great cooks, we don't care about paper; we care about plates. Plated and placed in front of you, it would be impossible to not tell these dishes apart. This is because each dish uses different herbs, spices, and seasonings.

The shawarma is full of warm cumin and curry flavors.

The shredded chicken tacos have hints of garlic and spiciness.

And the moo shu is both savory and sweet at the same time.

Effectively, three of the same dish done three different ways.

This is why developing our aromatic quality to the dish is so important. We do this by employing herbs and spices into our dishes to give them their distinct flavors.

I have a certain method to my madness when it comes to seasoning. I always season my dishes in a particular order: salty, savory, spicy, sour, and last sweet. But when it comes to adding aromatics, always add the stronger flavors that need to be extracted throughout the entire dish early in the cooking process. Stronger herbs and spices should always be added first.

A perfect example of this is rosemary. I love rosemary! Kept inside your house or outside, it will make your home smell amazing. Rosemary's natural scent acts as a stress reliever. So when I use rosemary in cooking, I always incorporate it early. The reason is that the aromatic quality of the rosemary is actually found in the oil contained within its needles. It is this scented oil that we are trying to incorporate throughout our entire dish. The best way to extract this is to smash the needles with a flat side of a knife and then incorporate it with hot oil. This will allow the oils to migrate out and co-mingle with the rest of the fats in the dish. This allows it to thoroughly coat every surface. We want to do this early when cooking a dish in order to give the rosemary time to not only be extracted but to mellow within the dish during the cooking process.

On the opposite end, there are herbs like basil. Basil has such a delicate flavor. Basil is such a tricky plant to use because if it is not quite right, you will completely loose the flavor from the basil leaves. In juxtaposition from the rosemary, if you add basil at any time but during the last few moments of cooking, the basil with become ethereal and disappear. Basil is a plant that should never be used as a dried herb. The essence of its flavor is best captured by using thinly sliced fresh leaves. It would preferably be added raw and not cooked. Think of a Caprese salad. The raw basil leaves give such a pop of flavor. This becomes the quintessential highlight of the dish. It pulls all the flavors together as if by magic.

So whenever we season with our aromatics, we want to first think:

1) When should I add this?
2) And how am I going to get the best flavor out of this ingredient?

A few examples of spices and herbs that should be added early are rosemary, cinnamon, cloves, nutmeg, peppers, and oregano.

Examples of spices and herbs that should be added last are basil, cilantro, parsley, orange blossoms, rose hips, and other lightly flavored seasonings.

Herbs and spices that fall in the middle are things like thyme, ginger, marjoram, cumin, and turmeric. These flavors don't really take time to develop and can therefore be added at anytime.

For your convenience, I have made a chart of commonly used spices and herbs, their flavors, functions, when they should be added to a dish, and what they are most commonly used with. This chart is found at the end of this book.

How To Combat Loss Of Appetite

Learning how to use the power of smell when cooking is probably the single most important part of cooking for any cancer patient going through chemotherapy. Followed by the concept of the palate cleanse. When a person eats food, drinks wine, or ingests any kind of substance, the strongest sense associated with this action is not taste but smell.

When I was learning how to cook, I worked for a chef. Let's call him "Big Chef." Big Chef and I worked at a golf course. We always had trouble getting customers to come eat in the morning. So to get people interested in our food, Big Chef would always have me cook up bacon in the morning. One day, I asked him why we did it. To me, it seemed like a waste to cook all that bacon if no one was going to eat it. What he explained to me was that the smell of the bacon would come out of the kitchen, go into the club house, up through the exhaust vents, and then finally out to the golf course itself. "You see. When people smell bacon, they can't help but get hungry. Somethin' about that bacon that makes people come a runnin'!" What I had yet to realize at the time was that your nose is so powerful it can govern your entire digestive system and ability to reason.

Let's once again use your dog as an example. If you start cooking bacon, where is your dog going to be? Right there next to you with the biggest set of eyes you've ever seen in your entire life! This is because that sense of smell they possess leads them right to the food every single time. We, as humans, like to feel detached from our animalistic senses. But, the truth of the matter is that regaining control of those senses becomes a very fundamental building block when we cook for cancer patients, especially chemotherapy patients.

Taste is a very basic sense. It only encompasses a few abilities for range and depth. For example: salty, savory, spicy, sour, and sweet. When you experience any other sensation besides these basic flavor and taste perceptions, it is smell or the nose of your food.

The advantage of using smell and targeting your cooking towards the nose is that

1) It gives you a wider breadth of experience while eating and

2) It allows you to build up the appetite of a cancer patient going through chemotherapy without actually putting food in front of them.

For example, when you have pot roast cooking in the oven, you can smell that the meat is slowly roasting. The fat melting and assimilating into the sauce and the muscle tissue. You can smell all of these things happening through your nose. You can begin to feel hungry without ever seeing the food in person. In dogs, the smell of food can be such a powerful sensation that a dog will salivate without ever seeing the food put in front of them.

How we use the power of smell is by using aromatic herbs and spices to trick someone's brain into being hungry. I know that in the case of my mom, I would use slowly sautéing garlic or mushrooms in olive oil or butter to illicit a hunger response.

The other thing we need to keep in mind when using smell is the adverse effect. You will remember this idea from earlier. It is called pungency.

Think about the most disgusting thing or food you have ever smelled. Maybe it made you feel physically ill. Maybe it was so gross that you actually did vomit? If you didn't have a sense of smell, that would never happen. On this point, we want to think about foods that your child will find smelly, stinky, or pungent and remove them when we are cooking. You will know this because you and your child will experiment together smelling everything and write it down as I had instructed you earlier in this chapter. This is where that road map starts to come into play.

During chemotherapy, my mom, who would normally be quite happy to scarf down a tuna salad sandwich, became physically ill if I even opened a can in a different room. Think about that. Your sense of smell is so powerful that a person can loose their appetite with out ever actually physically coming in contact with the item that causes the loss of appetite or nausea. This is why being conscious of smells is so important. To drive this point home even further, what you eat and cook for yourself, can have a direct effect on the hunger and ability to eat of a person who is fighting cancer. Talk about everybody and everything being interlinked. Isn't that crazy?

Here are some suggestions of food items that may smell delicious and illicit hunger in a cancer patient during chemotherapy

1) Sautéing any of the following in butter or olive oil

Garlic
Onions
Mushrooms
Green or Red Peppers

2) Grilling Meats

The smell of grilling meat has a primal effect on the human body. Examples of this would be, grilled chicken, seared steak, pan fried bacon.
Think about the kinds of foods that you and your family eat. What are the ones that your family gets excited about? If you can answer this question, you will be on the right path to re-building your child's hunger.

The following are food items that I would avoid during chemotherapy. Not because of the nutritional value of these food items but because of the smell. The smell of these food items may cause you to lose your appetite entirely.

1) Canned tuna/canned seafood
2) Soft mold ripened cheeses like Brie, Roquefort, Taleggio, etc.
3) Preserved and pickled foods like sourbraten, kimchi, pickled eggs, etc.
4) Stinky vegetables like cauliflower, cabbage, and broccoli

This by all means is not an all inclusive food list. Each person is different and will have different foods that they love and hate. Like I have said before in this book, each person is unique and as such will have unique reactions to every food. This list is better complied through experimentation than by simply just taking this list as gospel. In your tasting journal, write down and track what smells help make you hungry and what smells make you nauseous.

How To Combat Nausea

There are many well established ways to combat nausea that range from herbal traditional remedies to modern prescription medications. As I have taught you so far, there are sensory changes that occur during chemotherapy. We need to keep in mind how these changes can cause nausea. For ease and convenience, I have broken these various remedies and techniques down for you for personal consideration.

Combating Nausea the scientific way

Talk to your doctor about your nausea and more than likely they can prescribe a variety of medications that treat a variety of nausea intensities. When my mom went through chemotherapy treatments, she had two pills she could take: one for moderate nausea and one emergency pill for severe nausea. Remember though, that all medications have interactions and undesired side-effects. Make certain to cover these with your oncologist to choose the best selection.

Combating Nausea the traditional way

There are many options for herbal and folk remedies that have been time tested to combat mild nausea. Here are a few of my recommendations that worked for us.

1) Peppermint

It is available in tea and candy form. Peppermint has long been used as a folk remedy for nausea. I can say that it does work for mild to moderate nausea. For us, it seemed to be that the peppermint candies or breath mints worked a little better than the peppermint teas.

2) Ginger

A classic sore stomach soother. Ginger, which originated in east Asia, has been in use for thousands of years to sooth a sore stomach. It is available as a fresh root, a dried powder, a tea, or in soda form. Ginger does in fact work for mild to moderate nausea. Be warned in advance though, ginger is in fact a warm spicy flavor, not a mild sweet flavor. Its warm spicy flavor often takes people by surprise!

3) Sipping liquids

For mild nausea, a warm cup of soup broth to sip can help to set you right. In addition to this, soup broth has a caloric value which can be extremely helpful for those having trouble getting necessary nutrients into their bodies. You can also slowly sip water. This can help with mild nausea. Make certain not to quickly drink the liquids. An upset and sudden influx of fluids can cause the inverse of the intended effect and cause you to become extremely nauseous!

4) Rubbing alcohol *(isopropyl alcohol)*

This is a technique that a post-surgical nurse taught me. When you are extremely nauseous, take a cap full of rubbing alcohol and smell it. Do NOT snort it! Do NOT drink it! But take a few sniffs of the fumes. It will immediately settle your nausea. This technique does not work for everyone, but for those whom it works, it does work extremely well. I can personally vouch for this technique.

Techniques to avoid nausea entirely

As the old expression says "an ounce of prevention is worth a pound of cure." So, is this still true today? While not all nausea can be avoided, here are a few ideas and techniques that you can try to employ in your every day life.

1) Avoid pungent smells

Pungency is a concept that has to do with the strength of odors. Whereas smell describes the character of an odor. Pungency has to do with the strength irregardless of the pleasantry. For example, roses have a low pungency and it can be hard to detect their scent. Inversely, rotting fish has a very high pungency. Foods that have high pungency can induce nausea more easily than other foods.

2) Use soothing herbs in your cooking

Rosemary, sage, thyme, basil, parsley, and ginger all have soothing scents that can help to keep nausea from occurring while eating.

Hopefully these tips and techniques will get you started on the right path to not only combating nausea but avoiding it entirely.

How To Combat Mouth Sores

Mouth sores are an often reported and highly painful side effect of cancer and chemotherapy treatment. Mouth sores can be unavoidable as the chemotherapy begins to break down the softer tissues in your body. However, there are some good cooking techniques and tips to take into consideration so that we don't exacerbate mouth sores when eating.

1) Be conscious of heat both thermal and spicy

While it may be soothing to your throat to drink a nice hot cup of tea or broth, hot liquids can make mouth sores worse by burning the already irritated skin. This will set the healing process back and make it more difficult for your mouth sores to heal quickly.

I normally strongly espouse the use of spicy flavors in cooking. But when you have mouth sores, you want to be very careful with the amount of spiciness that you ingest during treatment. A touch of spice will naturally warm up a dish. However, if you add too much spicy, the burning sensation that spicy seasonings naturally impart in your food will physically burn the open sores in your mouth. This is not something you want, especially when dealing with all the other numerous treatment side-effects that occur. A quick tip to combat spicy flavors while you cook is to utilize vinegar to help cool down the spiciness of a recipe.

This is especially important to remember in kids who are fighting cancer. They usually do not have the same level of pain tolerance that an adult has. Any pain added can be excruciating. A perfect example of this are the ear infections that I used to get as a child. At the time, they seemed like the most painful thing that could ever possibly happen to me. But now, being an adult and having much better control of both my body and perception of pain, I am able to tolerate much more painful things on a daily basis.

Remember to keep in mind that everything that happens to a child, happens in a greater magnitude than to an adult. If mouth sores are aggressive, consider low temperature foods. What I mean by this is foods that can either be eaten at room temperature, refrigerator temperature, or freezer temperature. Because, hot foods can agitate mouth sores leading to an extremely painful experience.

2) Be texture conscious with your food

Dry foods like crackers, cookies, chips, and pretzels may taste delicious. But when you have mouth sores, they can be your worst enemy. The abrasive textures and rough edges of these foods can actually rub your mouth sores raw and make them worse. This can sometimes even lead to inadvertent bleeding!

You want to always ensure that all the foods you are eating are soft in texture while you have mouth sores. And while a nice toasted sub sandwich will sound amazing, the fallout from eating such a rough substance is sure to leave you in a raw situation.

With mouth sores, you really need to stick to soft non-abrasive textures. These don't have to be just soups and stews though. You can absolutely eat foods that are softer in texture like cold sandwiches, meals cooked in a slow cooker, pasta, mashed potatoes, smoothies, and the like.

3) Don't let your mouth become too dry

Use care when ingesting caffeine, salt, and acidic foods and liquids. While a nice cup of tea or your favorite cola drink may sound refreshing, the high acidity and caffeine can actually leave you more dehydrated than when you started. Salt, while it has many re-hydrating properties, can actually dry out your mouth if it is taken in excessive quantities.

Make certain to drink lots of fluids during cancer treatment. Don't make it difficult for your mouth to get hydration. The most logical way to stay hydrated is, of course, by ingestion. If possible, frequently sip water and rinse it around your mouth before swallowing. During my mother's cancer treatments, I would physically hold a cup of water with a straw for her to sip every hour to ensure she stayed properly hydrated.

You can also try an over the counter dry mouth rinse. Many oncologists will recommend a dry mouth rise for those with chronic dry mouth. These can help, but are not an end-all-beat-all solution to ending dry mouth. Many oncologists and cancer fighters report success with dry mouth rinses.

Other cancer fighters have reported success with a salt water rinse. Simply add a tablespoon of salt to 8 ounces of water and stir well. Rinse in your mouth like a mouth wash. Spit out the mixture when done. Do not swallow the salt water. It will make you ill.

Armed with this knowledge, you should be able to tackle mouth sores with no problem.

Inability To Chew Or Swallow

An inability to chew or swallow usually follows forms of head and neck cancer. The very first cooking question that I was ever asked in regards to cancer was about how to combat this problem. So, I feel it is very appropriate to include this information in my book just in case you find yourself in this situation.

Feeding a person who has difficulty chewing or swallowing may seem like an overwhelming task. But, the great news is we can fix this! The primary problems are usually lack of teeth, change in taste, and lack of saliva. What I would recommend are the following: soups, smoothies, and purees.

A puree is exactly what it sounds like. It is a fully cooked recipe introduced to a blender and liquefied. The good news is a puree tastes exactly like whatever food you made it out of. So, let's use baked potato soup for an example. You would make the baked potato soup as normal, which would normally be filled with big chunks of potato, bacon, and a hearty cream sauce. At this point, what you would do is either 1) use an immersion blender and puree the food inside of the pot *(like a marinara)* or 2) you remove some of the soup from the pot, add it to an external blender, and blend from there.

Two great things about purees are that 1) they taste exactly like whatever you made them out of and 2) you can alter the consistency. If your loved one is getting a bit of dry mouth, we can always add excess liquid to the puree to make it more runny. The trick to this though is not to loose flavor while you are watering it down. You still want it to taste good!

My advice on this would be to use whichever of the following ingredients is most appropriate in order to stretch out and moisten the recipe:

chicken broth
beef broth
vegetable broth

cream or whole milk
and other flavorful fluids that are similar to what you are preparing.

Always exchange like for like. IE: milk for cream, chicken broth for water, tomato sauce for tomato juice etc. As long as you follow the Roundness of Flavor techniques that are outlined in this book, you will end up with a flavorful product that is very satisfying.

The third great thing about purees is that they can be served hot or cold. Gazpacho is a perfect example of a cold puree. Purees were actually a very fancy way of preparing soups and side dishes in the early 1900's. The act of pulverizing a food product was thought to make digestion easier since it did not require any chewing but still maintained all of its nutritional value and fiber. There are tons of classical recipes for purees. You just might have to do some digging to find some recipes that you like.

The big key difference between a puree and baby food is adult flavor. Follow the *Roundness of Flavor* and *Palate Cleansing* techniques in this cookbook and you should have absolutely no trouble with this.

What Goes In, Must Come Out

Because we think of the body as a whole and all the systems as interlinked, let's discuss what happens after you get done eating and digesting. Yes, your assumptions are correct. We are going to talk about the big Number 2.

As the old saying goes, "what goes up, must come down." The same is true for eating, "what goes in, must come out." Normally, your body simply takes care of everything automatically. But, if you are going too much or going to little, it becomes quite the problem. I am going to give you some real world advice on these two common problems, address their causes, and offer you some helpful solutions that will hopefully enable you to rectify the situation quickly.

Let's first start with some basic biology. When you eat food or drink liquids, they travel through your mouth and into your stomach. After your stomach, they travel into your intestines. Eventually, all of this ends up at the other side coming out as Number 1 or Number 2. This is your body's way of eliminating waste and chemicals inside the body that have been converted. This is a super important function of your body. And if it doesn't work correctly, it can cause all kinds of other back ups in the system.

What's really interesting about digestion is that it is one of the core functions of your body. And yet, many people will go their entire lives without actually giving it any thought until there is a problem.

What To Do If There's No More 2

Generally speaking, an inability to go is caused by dehydration in the lower intestine. This could also be caused by not eating enough fiber or eating too much processed cheese. Other things that can stop you from going are the anesthesia used in surgery, opiate based narcotics found in pain pills, and many chemotherapy drugs will dry you out as well. An inability to go will cause pain, discomfort, bloating, and very stinky smells emanating from your behind. Two easy ways to start things up:

1) Increasing your fiber intake

Some examples of this would be fibrous vegetables like carrots, celery, mustard greens, radishes, and so much more. All plant material contains fiber. Fiber, as we call it, is actually cellulose. Cellulose makes up the cell walls of plants. This cellulose is what gives plants their firm texture and hardness. The more cellulose a plant contains, the harder it becomes. This is the reason we can build houses out of wood. Humans cannot properly digest cellulose. As a result, we call it indigestible fiber. This indigestible fiber is what pushes things along and acts like a binder for your food as it moves through your digestive track.

2) Increasing your hydration

The function of your lower intestine is to extract the water from your foods. If you're missing out on some daily commotion, it's a very good chance *(especially if you are on chemotherapy)* that your lower intestine has sucked all the water out of the food. This makes everything dry and painful. This also causes your waste to get stuck. The best solution I have found personally is good old fashioned, grandma approved, prune juice. I recommend drinking a glass or two. Give it some time to work its magic. Because when it works, IT WORKS! Prune juice is filled with all kinds of b vitamins, potassium, fiber, and a special naturally occurring chemical that will get things moving along fast. After the prune juice works it's magic, I recommend drinking a small glass of it a day to help with hydration and to continue to keep things moving.

What To Do If There's Too Much 2

Inversely, not being able to stop going can be just as bad, if not worse. The big concern with going too much is that it will cause rapid dehydration. This can lead to hospitalization. You simply do not want to get dehydrated. Going too much can be caused by a couple of things such as an inability to process whatever you have eaten. This can also be caused by something as dramatic as food borne illness or as simple as your body being unable to process a food item. This happens a lot to people who eat meats that are too heavy or try to eat uncooked veggies during chemotherapy treatment. I remember my mother really wanted a fresh leafy salad mid-way through chemotherapy. But, her body couldn't handle the uncooked foods and immediately her body rejected them. The result was the exact problem that we are addressing here. Going too much, can also be caused by cancer treatment drugs or a lack of dietary fiber in your diet. Here are some tips to help things from getting worse:

1) Drink plenty of fluids

Going too much, can cause rapid dehydration. This is an incredibly serious health problem. Don't just drink water. Water is actually not a very effective hydrator. Consider sports drinks, fruit juices, and cups of broth to keep your loved one hydrated. The additional salt found in these 3 items will help maintain the moisture in your body.

2) Increase your fiber

It may seem like the solution to both of these problems are identical. But, we are using them for different reasons. If you are going too much, increasing your fiber can help push out whatever it is your body is rejecting in the first place. This helps you to "dry up" faster.

3) Try over the counter medications like Imodium A-D

When my mom had this problem, Imodium really helped. I would recommend it as long as your doctor says that it is OK for you to use.

I never thought I would be talking about the other end of business inside of a cookbook. But with cancer patients, there are unique challenges. This, unfortunately, is one of them. Plus, I guess I am kind of the hero here because I have saved you from going into an online forum and having to ask these questions. Now you have solutions in the privacy and comfort of your own home and have maintained your dignity at the same time.

How To Cook For A Friend or Family Member That Has A Child Going Through Cancer Treatment

Cancer treatments don't just affect the people going through the treatments. A cancer diagnosis affects the family and friends of the person going through them as well. These friends very often want to step up and help their loved one get through such a hard time in their life. Most of the time, this type of support is received in the form of food donations to their loved one with cancer. And while these food donations are very much needed and incredibly helpful, there are a few things to take into consideration before baking your family member or friend a casserole. I have included this information so that you may share it with friends and family that want to help you and your family but don't know how. *(And haven't read this book.)*

Ask these question BEFORE you start cooking for your friend or family member's child.

1) Find out what foods their child is craving

Ask this child's parent if there are any foods or specific flavors that are easier for the child to eat or are there any foods that get them really excited about eating?

Cravings are a great thing! They are your body telling your brain how to vocalize the nutrients that your body is lacking. This expresses itself in many different forms from desiring big juicy cheeseburgers to baked beans to chocolate all the way to pickles. By embracing these cravings and catering to our loved ones preferences, we can help to ensure that they will get the nutrients that they need into them during cancer treatment. Remember that everybody is different and each craving will be different. Also, keep in mind that you are more likely to eat what you like than eat what you don't like.

2) Find out what foods or smells are making the child sick

Ask, "Are there any smells or specific foods that have been making your child nauseous?"

Nothing will turn a person off faster than foods that smell bad to them. An offensive smelling food will dry up someone's appetite faster than water in the desert. These offensive smells are known as pungent smells. We want to do our best to avoid them. If that is not possible, then we need to mask their smell. Broccoli is a major offender in the war against pungency. It is an incredibly healthy choice. But, often times its incorporation into a dish will make your loved one instantly nauseous from its pungent smell. If pungent smells cannot be completely avoided, they can be tempered with fragrant herbs and spices as well as incorporating 1 tablespoon of red wine vinegar followed by 1 tablespoon of sugar and cooked into the dish. The vinegar will neutralize the scent and the sugar will cover the taste and smell of the vinegar but still leave its special effects.

3) Remember to take the weight of the food into consideration

Ask your loved one, what types of foods has their child been having the most success with?

The reason we ask this is because heavier meats like chuck roast tend to be harder on the stomach than simple carbohydrates like rice. You need to know what kind of foods they have been having great success with. Then, you can make an informed decision on what foods to choose to cook for them. Heavier foods tend to lead to nausea where simpler foods do not.

4) Make food that is easily re-heated and easy to store

One of the best things you can do is to bring over pre-cooked and pre-portioned meals that can either be frozen or refrigerated and reheated quickly in the microwave or oven.

The reason we take this into consideration is that cancer is a time of high stress, high anxiety, and surprisingly tight schedules. Most people would assume that cancer treatment involved a lot of sitting around and recovering. When in fact, it is more likely that you will go to multiple specialists per week and be constantly on the run. Those few times that you do have a break, your body is so exhausted that all you can manage to do is sleep. We want our meals to be easily reheat-able and easily stored so that our loved ones can easily grab small bites of food when they have the energy to eat.

5) Think about texture

You should ask, are there any textures that are hurting their child's mouth. Another great question to ask is about the severity of dry mouth and mouth sores.

Mouth sores can be extremely painful to the point of where their debilitating effects cannot only break your spirit but also your ability to get nutritious meals into yourself. If mouth sores are really bad, consider meals that can be eaten at room temperature, like a cold soup. Other things you can do are to make sure you use soft textured food and avoid dishes that are overly spicy.

Armed with this information, you can make better choices and become a more effective contributor when you help your family and friends that are going through cancer treatments. Remember, when we cook for a loved one who is going through cancer treatment, we are NOT cooking for our preferences. We are cooking for their preferences.

CHAPTER 3:
BASIC INGREDIENTS AND KITCHEN EQUIPMENT

This chapter teaches you beginner kitchen knowledge. This is information you must know to have a more well-rounded view of cooking. In this chapter, you will learn what ingredients and spices you should always have on hand *(especially if you are cooking recipes from this book)*; kitchen equipment and utensils; clean versus sanitary; and how to properly prepare, cook, and store foods. All of this is super important because kids going through cancer treatment have compromised immune systems. You must learn how to properly handle food so that you don't accidentally give them food poisoning. Let's begin.

Basic Ingredients and Spices You Should Always Have In Your Kitchen

Since we've covered the basics of flavor, it's time to cover basic ingredients that you should always have in your kitchen and their uses. All of my recipes assume that you have the following ingredients in your pantry.

Ingredient Name	Flavor	Description
Kosher salt or course ground sea salt	salty	A very versatile salt, can be used to season a dish or as a marinade! The flakes are made especially for dissolving quickly and easily.
soy sauce	salty and savory	Fermented sauce made from wheat and soy. Buy a high quality soy sauce, as low quality and store brand soy sauce has an inferior flavor and tends to be bitter. I personally use the brand Kikkoman.
MSG	savory	Perfect savory amendment to any dish. It adds pizzazz to any dish or sauce. I recommend picking up a container or package of it at your local Asian market. It tends to be more reasonably priced. The two most common brands are Accent and Aji-No-Moto.
black pepper *(fine ground)*	spicy	Most common of all peppers. Great in anything. Most commonly used as table pepper.
red pepper	spicy	Available as ground or flakes. A spicy pepper that adds a nice kick to dishes.
cayenne pepper	spicy	Normally sold as ground cayenne pepper. Hot but subtle. NOTE: Unlike other flavors that mellow or temper with longer cooking, cayenne pepper is unique in that the longer you cook it the spicier it becomes.

red wine vinegar	sour	Great vinegar for most anything. Adds a nice clean taste to dishes.
rice vinegar	sour	Traditionally used in Asian cooking. It is sweeter than its western counterpart.
lemon juice	sour	Acidic juice from lemons pre-squeezed. Great on seafood and Mediterranean dishes.
lime juice	sour	Acidic juice from limes pre-squeezed. Full of vitamin C. Great for tropical, Caribbean, and Central American dishes.
granulated sugar	sweet	Regular old sugar. Extremely versatile. Can be used for sweetening, baking, mixing into coffee, really whatever you need sugar for!
pure olive oil	fatty	Great healthy oil with a low smoke point. This is good for healthy low temperature sauteing.
extra virgin olive oil	fatty	Great healthy oil for use in non-cooked dishes. The biggest difference between extra virgin olive oil and pure olive oil is that extra virgin olive oil is green. It is used only in fresh dishes and is more expensive than pure olive oil. Extra virgin olive oil is a ready to eat food and is not suitable for cooking.
vegetable oil	fatty	Usually made from soy beans. It has a high smoke point making it ideal for frying or sauteing.
butter	fatty	You will notice my recipes always call for butter over margarine. Butter is natural, contains calcium, and makes everything taste amazing. If desired, you may substitute margarine for butter in equal amounts.
wheat flour	starchy	Great for baking or thickening sauces.
corn starch	starchy	Perfect for thickening sauces or creating crispy crusts on deep fried items.

On MSG (Mono Sodium Glutamate)

There is a lot of controversy surrounding MSG and whether it is good for you, bad for you, or neutral. I would like to clarify exactly what it is, how it is made, and the honest truth behind it. I would like to state that I personally use MSG and see no problems cooking with it whatsoever.

From the USDA: "...MSG is the sodium salt of glutamic acid. Glutamic acid is an amino acid, one of the building blocks of protein. It is found in virtually all food and, in abundance, in food that is high in protein, including meat, poultry, cheeses, and fish."

What MSG does is provide a chemical called glutamate to your tongue. Glutamate is a naturally occurring organic chemical that tells your brain, "This is savory, rich, and delicious." Glutamate occurs naturally in all foods we eat and cook with, except for ones that are not derived from plants, animals, or fungi. Some examples of foods with highly concentrated deposits of glutamate are: anchovies, kelp, red wine, green tea, soy sauce, meats, poultry, and mushrooms.

MSG was discovered by Japanese researcher Kikunae Ikeda in 1908 by creating a crystalline extract of glutamic acid from seaweed. Sometime in the 1920s, Dr. D.Y. Chow, from the National Dyes Company of Hong Kong, developed the process for extracting MSG from wheat. This is how it is still produced today. *(Reference: The Wok, by Gary Lee, Nitty Gritty Cookbooks)* The main problem with MSG is that people use too much in their cooking, because quite frankly it makes everything instantly delicious!

MSG by itself has very little flavor aside from the instant savory feeling in your mouth. But when applied with salt, it becomes a flavor explosion! The problem here as you can see, is you end up saturating your food with sodium. Sodium can be disastrous for someone with heart disease or high blood pressure. So when I cook and intend to use MSG in addition to salt, I reduce the amount of salt to allow for the extra sodium contained in the MSG.

The only known side effect to MSG is occasionally it will cause headaches in certain people. Now remember, this is a super small group of people who have any kind of adverse reaction. If these people were truly allergic to glutamate, they would have headaches anytime they ingested foods that naturally have high concentrations of glutamate. ie: chicken, fish, beef, etc. I personally think that it is the additional amount of sodium causing the headaches in salt-sensitive people. Or, more than likely, it is a slight dehydration experienced from too much sodium intake.

A good rule of thumb with MSG is to use no more than 2 percent of the weight of the recipe. The most ground breaking part of MSG is that you can make entirely meatless broths that taste amazing. ie: hot and sour soup, egg drop soup, miso soup, vegetarian vegetable soup, etc. This is especially helpful for vegetarians and vegans who are having trouble making their food taste great!

So don't be afraid to put MSG in your food, especially when fighting cancer. My point of view is that anything we can do to get food into your loved ones is an improvement. I found that adding a little bit of extra sugar and MSG to my mom's foods kept everything down and got her to go back for seconds!

MSG is typically marketed as "Essence of Umami," "Umami Extract," "Umami Seasoning," or some variation on the word "Umami." Umami is the Japanese word for savory, as the researchers who discovered the sense of savory on your tongue were Japanese.

If you would like some evidence that the MSG scare is still alive and well in peoples consciousness, simply go to your local grocery store, Asian market, or Asian restaurant. You will readily find packages and signs proudly proclaiming "NO ADDED MSG." They have to say NO "ADDED" MSG because glutamic acid is a naturally occurring substance found in almost all food. I am not trying to convince you to put MSG into all of your food. I am simply suggesting it as a supplemental weapon to fight the side-effects from cancer treatment.

Now if you are still scared of MSG, you can absolutely go the long way around and add some of the other examples I've listed to make your food more savory. *(anchovies, mushrooms, bay leaves, soy sauce, Parmesan cheese, tomatoes, etc.)* But, it will take longer, generally cost more, and will require more product weight to make the same flavor. If your remember, the purpose of this cookbook is to make your life as easy as possible. I can make sauces, gravies, and dishes incredibly savory, decadent, and delicious without the addition of glutamate extract. I just simply don't want you living in fear of MSG because the health food movements surrounding cancer are full of lies, deceit, and deliberate misinformation.

Trust me on this one. Buy MSG from your local Asian Market. It will be much cheaper than any other store. For more great reading on Mono Sodium Glutamate, I recommend reading "It's the Umami, Stupid. Why the Truth About MSG is So Easy to Swallow" by Natasha Geiling, featured in Smithsonian Magazine's website November 8th, 2013.

Kitchen Equipment and Utensils

Not all equipment is created equal! The first thing you should know about kitchen equipment is that price does not always dictate quality. In home goods, most items are priced based on the brand name, color, and material they are made of. If you can get your hands on a good set of restaurant grade equipment at your local restaurant supply company, you will be all the happier for it! Restaurant grade equipment is about the same price as medium-level home goods, but the quality and construction are much higher and can tolerate much more abuse! Having worked in restaurant kitchens, you wouldn't believe the amount of times I have watched a cook try to destroy a restaurant grade sauté pan simply because they were angry. And the sauté pan suffered little to no actual damage.

I recommend the following kitchen equipment

8 inch sauté pan
12 inch sauté pan
1 gallon pot
2 quart sauce pan
4 quart sauce pan
rice cooker *(One that holds at least two cups but no larger than eight cups.)*
colander
whisk
potato masher
high temperature spatula
high temperature plastic flipper
high temperature plastic spoon
metal flipper

metal tongs

flat-bottomed wok

1/2 pan baking sheet

a set of ceramic or glass casserole dishes

8 inch chef's knife

6 inch boning knife

paring knife

a pull through knife sharpener

bacteria-resistant cutting board

good kitchen towels

pot holders

measuring cups

measuring spoons

digital kitchen scale

can opener

handy-dandy kitchen thermometer

You don't have to have all of this equipment. But with all of this, you can make pretty much anything. You always want to make certain that all of your equipment is clean, operable, and in good working order.

How To Select Kitchen Equipment

So now that you have a list of kitchen equipment. Let me teach you the subtle differences in kitchen equipment so that you know what to look for when you are at the store.

The Difference Between Pots and Pans

Shopping for pans is like shopping for a car. Everybody has their own opinion as to which brand is best. Some like Chevy. Some like Ford. And others, they prefer a BMW. The best advice I can give you is to break down the differences in materials and their benefits. From there, it's about thickness, personal preference, and application.

There are 3 common materials that pans are commonly made out of. They are iron, steel, and aluminum. Let's explore in greater detail below.

Iron pans tend to be thick, very heavy, and heat evenly but very slowly. Iron can also be extremely durable. For example, I have a cast iron skillet from my great-grandmother that I still use often. It is at the very least 50 to 60 years old. The advantage to iron is that, not only is it durable, but iron heats extremely uniformly and will retain heat upon application of food product. This makes a cast iron skillet an ideal choice when you need to sauté or braise your food with high heat and maintain the temperature. Another advantage of iron is its' consistent cooking temperatures. It is extremely easy to prepare food and maintain the pan at the desired cooking temperature. The disadvantages to iron are that 1) It is difficult to maintain as you must use a special washing process and oil the metal after each use. And 2) It is very heavy in weight, making it hard to perform simple tasks like sauteing and flipping with a wrist action. I recommend everyone own at least one cast iron skillet in their collection. I forgot to mention that iron pans taste better with age as they tend to "season" with the natural oils of the foods you cook in them.

Steel is a good metal for making cookware. It is very durable and heats very nicely. But like iron, it is very heavy and heats very slowly. Steel does not need the same level of care as iron cookware, as steel tends to be stainless, or no rust. This makes it an ideal choice as a replacement for iron, if you don't want to do all the maintenance. I like to think of steel cookware as the everyday version of iron cookware.

Aluminum cookware is the absolute opposite of iron. It heats very quickly. It is very light and is the most common of all cookware materials. The biggest disadvantage to aluminum is scorching. Since the aluminum heats so quickly, it is prone to scorching your meals. The aluminum metal tends to be very thin. The aluminum also heats inconsistently and pans will tend to have hotter and cooler spots when you cook with them. When you buy aluminum cookware, thickness is the key. The thicker the pan, the more material that has to be heated. As such, it provides a more even distribution of heat. This leads to more even cooking temperatures and better tasting food. Aluminum is my choice for everyday cookware. Since the aluminum is lighter than steel, using a wrist flipping action is less stressful to your wrists. This allows for less tiring cooking sessions.

How To Buy Pots and Pans

Now that we know about the materials. Lets discuss how to buy them.

When you search for new cookware, no matter what material you buy, you want to look at 2 items:

1) the thickness of the material

2) the handles

Thicker materials are always better. A thicker metal will always heat more evenly and lead to less burning than a thin metal. Always compare like to like when choosing between two sets of cookware. Always compare steel to steel, aluminum to aluminum, and iron to iron.

When buying new cookware, you always want to consider the handles' comfort when you hold it. Ask yourself: "Is this handle something I can hold in my hand for 30 to 60 minutes comfortably?" Also keep in mind that a cheap handle will begin to jiggle after a few uses. If you are me, the jiggling will drive you crazy.

When I buy cookware, I try to buy items that have been NSF certified. This tends to indicate *(but not always)* a more commercial grade of cookware. NSF means "National Safety Foundation." It is a third-party safety and quality verifier in the United States. NSF certification may not be available in all countries. Commercial cookware tends to be of a more durable make, but that is not always the case. Some high end cookware for personal use is of a much higher construction quality than cheaper commercial cookware.

As far as Teflon vs no Teflon goes, I personally like a coated pan. BUT, you have to make sure that it is not a cheap Teflon coating. Teflon is safe to cook with but can be highly cancerous if ingested. So always throw away pans that have a Teflon coating if they begin to peel. A good alternative to this is a quality ceramic coating. Ceramic coatings tend to be a little more expensive. But, they can be worth it. Remember, as with all things in life, you get what you pay for. Wash all Teflon coated pots and pans with a soft non abrasive cloth and mild soap. As a last thought, you never ever want to use metal utensils on Teflon coated pans as they are guaranteed to scratch the Teflon coating after a few uses.

In conclusion, the choice is ultimately up to you. But, I hope this has given you a road map to buying new equipment. Ultimately, the decision is yours. But with trial and error, you will learn what equipment works best for you. Once you learn what your personal preferences are, you will be able to make more informed decisions. As with all things, practice makes perfect!

My last thought on cookware is that the experience level of the cook is the ultimate deciding factor on whether or not the cookware will work for your application. An experienced cook can make low-quality cookware work for them. And an inexperienced cook can still ruin a dish in a $150 sauté pan.

Just remember, there is no such thing as a "good" cook or a "bad" cook. There are only varying levels of experience and knowledge!

Quick Kitchen Equipment Maintenance Tips

You should always throw away any pots or pans with Teflon that is peeling. If you have any Teflon coated pans, there is a proper way to maintain them. Never ever use an abrasive scrubbing pad on them. Always use a soft rag and mild soap to clean them. Never drop a hot pan or pot into cold water as it will warp the pan. Iron skillets should never be washed in the dish washer. Instead, wash them by hand, dry immediately, and apply a thin coat of oil on the surface to keep the iron from rusting. On wooden utensils: If you prefer wooden utensils, I completely sympathize. But, you must take great care to sanitize the utensils properly. Bacteria can build up in the wood's natural crevices. So, be smart, clean, and careful.

Knives

I want to talk a little more in depth about knives. Knives are an essential but dangerous tool that we use every day in kitchens. There are right ways and wrong ways to handle, clean, and carry a knife. When you handle a knife, you should always keep a firm grip on the handle. If the knife is large, like a chef's knife, you should choke-up on the handle like a baseball bat. I handle my chef's knife by placing the blade through my index and middle finger. Then, I pull my fingers flat against the sides of the blade. Never overlap the actual cutting part. Then, you grip the handle with the rest of your fingers firmly. If you do it like this, you will have great control and accuracy. You will be less likely to cut yourself. When you cut, make certain to pull your finger tips, on your holding hand, away from the cutting blade. Make a flat surface to cut against with your knuckles. This ensures that you will have accuracy and control!

When you clean a knife, always do it by hand. Never leave a knife in the sink! A knife in a sink is an accident waiting to happen! When you carry your knife around the kitchen, make sure that the flat part of the blade is parallel and close to your body. The point should be facing down, and the blade pointed backward. If you ever hand someone a knife, hand it to them handle first.

The last rule on knives is to always keep them as sharp as possible! Not only is a sharp knife easier to work with, but it is also actually safer to work with. The reason for this is simple. A sharp knife requires less strength to cut into objects. Therefore, it is less likely to pass through the object and then into your skin. If the knife does end up cutting your skin, a cut from a sharper blade is less jagged and will remove less material in your skin. This allows for less pain and a quicker recovery! So, go out and buy yourself a pull through knife sharpener. You'll thank me for it later!

CHAPTER 4:
FOOD SAFETY

Clean vs. Sanitized

There is an old saying: "Cleanliness is next to godliness." This saying is very true when you are cooking. It is especially true when you are cooking for people undergoing chemotherapy. Their immune systems are suppressed. This makes them more susceptible to sickness from food. So, make certain that you thoroughly sanitize every surface in your kitchen every time you begin cooking, switch tasks, and finish cooking!

To conclude the point: clean, clean, clean, clean!

Now before I go any further, I must explain to you that there is a difference between something that is clean and something that is sanitized.

The simplest way to explain this is: Clean is an aesthetic quality. Sanitized is science.

For example, just because something looks clean, does not mean it is sanitized and germ free. Let's say I just cut up uncooked chicken on my counter. Then, I wiped off any juice with a dry towel. The surface now looks clean, but the germs and bacteria from the uncooked chicken are still on the counter even though you can't see them. This is actually one of the easiest ways to get food poisoning.

Another way to think about clean is to think about home design shows on HGTV. They'll describe a brand new modern layout as having clean lines. "Clean" in this context actually refers to the minimalist qualities of that design.

Sanitary, on the other hand, is a scientific state. The ugliest item in your home can be made sanitary. What we mean by sanitary is "free of bacteria, viruses, allergens, and dirt."

Now when you sanitize a surface, you are decontaminating it or killing any bacteria or germs that you can or cannot see. You sanitize by using a liquid solution that kills germs and bacteria. Everyone has their own preference. But, the point you need to take away is that is has to be a solution that kills bacteria!

This is how we do it in restaurants. We use a solution that is called Sani-Water to wipe tables and kitchen surfaces. It is a mixture of bleach and water. It is a measurement of 1 tablespoon of bleach to one gallon of hot water. This will yield the desired 200 ppm solution. Doing something as simple as adding bleach to the water will kill all the bacteria and germs on surfaces. Just like adding chlorine to a pool prevents germs from growing in a public pool. If you want to use the bleach and water method, follow the directions on the bottle to achieve the desired results.

Every time you 1) switch tasks or 2) touch raw or uncooked food, you must always sanitize your kitchen surfaces and wash your hands with soap and water to help prevent cross-contamination.

Cross-Contamination

Cross-contamination is simply what happens when you contaminate an item through one of the following conditions:

1) not properly sanitizing a surface
2) accidentally carrying over material from another task or
3) forgetting to wash your hands before beginning your next task

What we mean by switching tasks is if you are cutting onions and switch to potatoes, this would not be switching tasks as they both have the same type of bacteria. But if we switch major tasks, like cutting chicken, and then switching to raw potatoes, we need to sanitize in between. When we prepare items, to keep it as sanitary as possible, we start by preparing items with the lowest temperature required to kill bacteria in it, working up to the highest.

Refer to the chart in the *Properly Preparing, Cooking, and Storing Food* section for proper cooking temperatures and the proper refrigerator storage method to help avoid contamination.

The three easiest ways to get food poisoning are by:

1) not washing your hands
2) not properly sanitizing surfaces before switching tasks *(cross-contamination)*
3) not cooking or reheating your food to the proper temperature

Also, I hope most of you know this. But, just in case I will remind you. Never ever let cooked ready to eat food touch uncooked food. I cannot say this enough. Sanitize your surfaces. Wash your hands. Sanitize your surfaces. Wash your hands. And just to drive the point home one last time to make sure you fully understand the high importance of this lesson. **SANITIZE YOUR SURFACES AND WASH YOUR HANDS!**

Properly Preparing, Cooking, and Storing Food

There is a proper method and order to preparing food that you intend to use, eat, or cook later. The first thing we want to think about is cross-contamination. As we just learned, cross contamination occurs when bacteria from one food item moves to another. This is especially dangerous when it is bacteria that dies at a higher cooking temperature than what the food will be prepared at.

So with this in mind, we will apply the cross-contamination knowledge to how we prepare food. Whenever you are making a dish, for ease and convenience, it is always best to prepare the items you intend to cook ahead of time. Then, place them in sealed storage containers for later use. If you find you are running out of time to make meals, you can always pre-slice or pre-cut up any vegetables you will need throughout the week and store them in the refrigerator for later use.

We had some days that were busy with treatments and doctor visits. And, we had some days where there would be nothing going on. So, I would keep my refrigerator stocked with ready-to-use food items. Some vegetables can also be frozen very easily. Simply slice them up, put them in freezer safe bags, and freeze them. This is especially helpful if you are not consuming your fresh food products as fast as they are going bad. Feel free to experiment and find veggies that work well for you. If you do freeze them, you do have to cook them. Frozen vegetables loose their structure and become incredibly soft after being frozen. This shouldn't be to much of an issue though. It is generally recommended that people with compromised immune systems only eat fully cooked foods. With all these things in mind, let's talk about the proper order to prepare, or prep, for a meal.

We want to prepare all of our food items in this order:

Food Preparation Chart

Order Of Preparation When Cooking	Item To Be Prepared
first	fruits and vegetables
second	ready to eat items or items that will be eaten raw
third	dairy
fourth	seafood
fifth	red meats and pork
last	poultry

Fruits and Vegetables

The proper way to prepare fruits and vegetables is as follows: You want to first thoroughly wash any contaminates away, like dirt, to ensure that no contaminates are present during ingestion. We do not want to remove the skins of thinly skinned foods. The skins contain lots of vitamins, minerals, and extra fiber. Slice to desired size. Next, we will place the vegetables in sealed containers for storage.

Ready-To-Eat Foods

Ready-to-eat foods are very simple. But, there are few things you need to make sure you take care of to avoid cross-contamination. First, keep ready-to-eat foods in their own container and away from any raw meats. The next thing we need to think about is reheating temperature. This is incredibly important for ready-to-eat foods. If it's yogurt and it's suppose to be cold, it always needs to be under 40°F. If the ready-to-eat food is supposed to be served hot, it needs to be brought to 145°F before serving. This will kill any bacteria that may have formed in the food since its packaging. A note on pre-made soups: I find that canned, broth-based soups taste a little better if you bring them to a boil for a few minutes before serving.

Dairy

Dairy items are usually ready to eat in the condition that they are in. But, we need to make sure that they are always stored at 40°F or lower until it is time to consume them. We also need to be careful because dairy products like yogurt and cheese contain active bacteria cultures. This is what gives them their unique and special flavors. We just need to make sure that this friendly bacteria doesn't turn into harmful bacteria. We do this by properly storing and keeping dairy items separate from other items.

Meat

We want to keep all meat separate from each other, as well as all of the other food groups. At the very least, they all contain some level of bacteria on their surface. The exceptions to this are ground meats and chicken. Those meats have a uniform bacterial disbursement throughout their structure. The reason for this has to do with the specific nature of the processing of those foods in the United States. I can't speak to how other countries process their meat, but this is something that needs to be taken into consideration.

To prepare meats ahead of time, we can cut, season, or prepare these items up to three days in advance if it is going to sit in the refrigerator at 40°F or lower. Or, it can sit in the freezer for an indefinite amount of time. This is assuming they are packaged properly to prevent freezer burn.

If we do prepare our meats ahead of time, we want to make sure they are in their own containers or storage bags that are properly sealed. If preparing several different meats at once, take care to clean your cutting board, knives, and surfaces inbetween each task. And remember to always cut items in the above preferred order to help avoid unnecessary cross-contamination.

Properly Cooking Food

Remember that when you cook meats for cancer patients that are going through treatment, the meat needs to be well done. This is to make certain that any bacteria are dead as a door nail! Well-done temperatures will vary per meat category:

Proper Cooking Temperatures Chart

Meat Item	Cook To Temperature
chicken, turkey, and poultry	165°F
beef, pork, veal, and lamb	155°F
fish, shrimp, other seafood, and veggies	145°F

You need to hold these temperatures for at least 30 seconds to make sure everything is nice and safe to eat. You can find the temperature with a handy-dandy kitchen thermometer. If you don't have one, I highly recommend that you purchase one!

The temperatures listed above are the prescribed temperatures as recommended by the USDA. These temperatures are almost always in constant flux. So double check with the USDA website to make sure that these are still the current correct well-done temperatures.

Raw Vegetables

At this point, I think it would be prudent to discuss raw veggies. There is no effective way to decontaminate raw veggies with any accuracy or effectiveness. Because of this, I would not feed any kids going through cancer treatment raw veggies or raw fruit. Especially, if they have a compromised immune system. This is simply a better safe than sorry technique that I take. It only takes a few bacteria getting into your body to give you violent food poisoning. This causes diarrhea, vomiting, and generally making someone who is already fighting cancer have to fight even harder for no reason. Diarrhea and vomiting can cause extreme dehydration. This can cause death in children. Food poisoning is simply not worth the risk. I know that about halfway through chemo, my mom was craving a salad. I eventually caved-in and prepared one for her. Unfortunately, her body simply couldn't process the raw greens. Her body then rejected the salad. There are still many ways to work fruits and veggies into meals. So, don't lose hope that you won't be able to make complete and healthy meals full of vitamins and minerals! If you have trouble getting complete vitamins, minerals, and nutrients into your meals, you can always use supplements. You can also get protein and fiber supplements if necessary as well. ALWAYS talk to your doctor and dietitian first before making any changes of this kind.

Properly Storing Food

Storage of foods can be just as important as keeping your work space clean. You want to refrigerate everything at a temperature under 40°F. Refrigerate or freeze all fresh foods immediately when you get them home. If you won't use raw meat right away, just freeze it. It is better to loose a little flavor for overall food safety when cooking for children with compromised immune systems.

Make certain that all leftovers are placed in sealed containers and cooled down as fast as possible. Leftovers are usually good to eat for seven days after preparation. If you want to store food for longer than that, just freeze it!

The seven-day rule can be trumped by the "nose test." If it smells stinky and it shouldn't, don't risk it. Just pitch it!

Proper stacking order in your fridge should be just like we are strictly required by law to keep in a restaurant.

Proper Storage and Drip Method Chart

Shelf Level	What Goes On Each Shelf
top shelf	ready-to-consume foods: raw fruits, vegetables, or pre-cooked foods
top-middle shelf	dairy products or anything with a live active bacteria culture: yogurt, salami, cheese
bottom-middle in this order	raw seafood, beef, pork, veal, red meats
bottom shelf	Raw poultry, chicken

Home refrigerators are actually built backward from how we are legally required to store food in a restaurant. How they can get away with this, I don't know. Home fridges are designed for space not cleanliness. And that is just the wrong way to do it.

There is a proper method to store your foods in your refrigerator and freezer. It is called the "drip method." For example, if a slice of carrot drips down into raw chicken, cooking the chicken at the proper temperature of 165°F will kill any bacteria that the carrot could have contributed. The idea is that any leaking fluids or any downward cross-contamination would naturally be wiped out by cooking the food to the proper temperature.

For instance, the reason that we cook seafood to 145°F is because the types of bacteria that naturally occur in these organisms die by 145°F. The bacteria that naturally occurs in beef *(E.coli)* is a naturally occurring intestinal bacteria found in cows, that aides in digestion, and is dead as a door nail by 155°F. So if a little E.coli ends up in our chicken, and we cook our chicken to 165°F, that E.coli has long since been passed for at least 10°F. If the reverse were to happen and the naturally occurring salmonella in the chicken ends up in our seafood. It is only cooked to 145°F. So, the fish will still be full of live active salmonella. This will result in an incredibly unpleasant bathroom experience.

Remember, children have weaker immune systems than adults. A disease that wouldn't even cause an adult to have the sniffles can render a child completely bed ridden. To drive this point home even further, think about how many children your great grandparents had. It's usually some astronomical number like 13, 14, or 15 kids. But, only 5 of them survived to adulthood. This is because children do not have the resistance or immunity to disease like an adult has. Resistance simply develops over time. This is why avoiding food poisoning is so important. Wouldn't it destroy you for the rest of your life if the reason that your child died was because you didn't cook their chicken long enough? I know it's very scary but that is the level of terrified that you should be of food poisoning when your child has cancer.

Defrosting Frozen Food

There are two sure-fire ways to defrost foods and not get sick:
1) place whatever the frozen item is in the fridge two days before use
2) defrost in cold, running water

To use the running water method, place food item in an air-tight bag and place in a bowl. Fill the bowl with cold water. Allow a trickle of cold water to run from the faucet into the bowl continuously. This allows even heat exchange. Also the fresh water will prevent bacterial build up.

I do not recommend this method unless you seal the item in a bag for two reasons:
1) it is very easy to cross-contaminate your food
2) the water will wash away the natural flavors of the food

Another method I use is specifically for ground meat and frozen veggies. I place my frozen ground beef in a covered sauté pan. I make sure to cover the beef in water. Then, I place it on high heat and cook the meat while defrosting it. Your meat won't be in the danger zone *(41–144°F)* for long enough to grow any bacteria. It's also much faster than waiting for it to defrost! This is a perfect defrosting method when you need a cooked ground meat as main ingredient like in tacos or spaghetti bolognese.

CHAPTER 5:
BASIC NUTRITION

Introduction to Nutrition

Nutrition is a relatively new idea in the medical community. Nutrition is also an incredibly dry and boring subject that even my wife Jessie, that helps me write all my books and articles, routinely looses her attention span and possibly even consciousnesses while discussing. Because she is my litmus test on what the average person has the attention span to understand and enjoy, I will try my best to keep this section as brief, entertaining, and to the point as possible.

Before we get too much into nutrition, I have to define what a nutritionist and registered dietitian are.

Nutritionist: In the USA, a nutritionist is a person who offers advice to people on nutritional information. This is a self-appointed title and their actual experience and knowledge can vary widely. Be warned, there is no standardization to this title and no testing or accreditation associated with it. Many people become nutritionists when they become personal trainers or fitness instructors. This isn't to say that all nutritionists are unqualified or should not be listened to. Many have the best intentions at heart. But, use caution and common sense when speaking to a nutritionist, simply because they are not medical professionals.

Registered Dietitian: A registered dietitian is a medical professional who is very similar to a nutritionist in their function. In some countries, the word nutritionist is interchangeable with dietitian. A registered dietitian is an expert in nutrients, diets, is certified, and often an employee of a hospital. To be a registered dietitian, you have to have a degree in dietetics and pass a licensing exam. Because of this, dietitians will have a specialty just like any other health care professional. The one you will see most often with cancer treatment is an oncological dietitian. You can identify a dietitian because they will often bare the initials RD LD behind their name. Because dietitians go through a fairly standardized training, they will tend to give you similar advice based on your situation. I do recommend working with a dietitian in conjunction with your oncologist. They can help make certain that you are getting all of the necessary nutrients that your body needs to heal quickly and properly.

Nutrition, in addition to being an incredibly boring topic, is also an incredibly personal topic. Because everyone's body is different, everyone will have different successes and failures with different types of foods and food groups. You must treat your diet uniquely and not blindly follow other peoples advice. You are your own best advocate. No one dietary regime will work for everyone. I especially urge you to use caution if you are deciding to try a new dietary program during cancer treatment. A drastic change in your diet can come as a shock to your system and can cause you further complications. Any changes that you do make in your diet should be introduced slowly. So, I guess what I am saying here is don't try to get fancy. Remember that you already have cancer. Our first objective is to get rid of that cancer. Once your cancer has entered remission, that's when we can try to get fancy and switch things around. I also strongly advise you to work with your dietitian and your doctor to come up with a nutritional plan that works best for you.

There is a lot of misinformation when it comes to food and its relationship to cancer. I need to set your expectations correctly. To date, the only proven treatments for cancer, that I am aware of, are chemotherapy, radiation, and immunotherapy. But to set your expectations correctly, you need to know that food, no matter what you eat, will not cure your cancer. It doesn't matter how much raw food you eat, leafy greens, gluten-free, or whole foods. Food simply does not cure cancer. It is not that I wish to take your hope from you. I simply wish to be realistic with you that there is no miracle cure for cancer. If there was, you could patent it and sell it for any price that you wanted and be the richest person on earth. Remember, cancer is not one disease. It is a group of related diseases. This is the reason why treatment for cancer varies based on the disease.

Now that I have set your expectations correctly, I do need to say that nutrition is important. Nutrition is especially important during cancer treatment. What you eat when you are sick determines your ability to rebuild damaged cells. In the case of children, it determines their ability to continue to grow and develop. Kids need healthy protein, vitamins and minerals, carbohydrates, healthy fats, and fiber in their diet so that they can grow big and strong. This is also important so that their body can heal during and after cancer treatment. Cancer treatment can be very hard on your child's body. So in the rest of this section, I am going to teach you about macro nutrients and a simplified nutritional theory that will make getting healthy rounded meals into your child a breeze.

Introduction to Macro Nutrients

Macro nutrients are large categories of nutrients that our bodies need to continue existing. When we make meals, we need to make certain that we get all of these nutrients into our bodies to the best of our abilities. One of the best ways to do this is by planning meals that get a little bit of the food guide pyramid into each meal. If you are not familiar with the food guide pyramid, simply search google for "food guide pyramid." It is almost always the first result. Because cancer treatment is so hard on the body, you need to make sure that your kids are getting plenty of protein, vitamins, and minerals.

Now that we are familiar with the food guide pyramid, we are going to simplify the concept and categorize it into three easy to understand categories.

1) **Proteins and fats** are grouped into one group because they normally run hand in hand. It is easier to manage fat intake by choosing good, healthy sources of lean meats. Foods that are higher in protein than other nutritional sources *(like calcium)* were placed into this category as well. This is why I categorize dairy into this category as opposed to giving it its own category.

Lean proteins have a lower fat content in them than other protein sources. That is why they are called *lean* proteins. It is easy to over cook these lean proteins which will make them dry and difficult to chew. Another reason, I recommend lean proteins is simply because fatty meats, while more tender, can be heavier on a cancer fighters stomach. This is especially true if they are going through intensive chemotherapy.

Examples include: beef, chicken, pork, lamb, veal, fish, eggs, beans, legumes, lentils, tofu, chickpeas, milk, cheese, soy milk, meat substitutes, etc.

2) **Carbohydrates** are a simplified group that usually includes starches *(complex carbohydrates)*, sugars *(simple carbohydrates)*, and non-digestible fiber *(super-complicated carbohydrates)*. Any food that provides more carbohydrate value than other nutrients *(enriched wheat flour)* was placed into this group.

Examples include: wheat, barley, pasta, rice, breads, potatoes, cereal, granola, etc.

3) **Vitamins and minerals** are the category for all foods that don't fall into the other two categories. Primarily, I intend it to reference fruits and vegetables. Fruits and vegetables are some of the best sources of essential vitamins and minerals.

Examples include: fruits, vegetables, juices, supplements, etc.

Why do we need these nutrients in our diet?

Proteins and Fats

What we call proteins are actually a group of macro nutrients that are made up of amino acids. There are two kinds of amino acids: essential and non-essential. Essential amino acids must be obtained by eating because the human body cannot produce them on its own. Non-essential amino acids can be produced by your body naturally. Proteins are used for immune function, tissue repair, growth, making hormones, making enzymes, preserving muscle mass, and helps you rebuild your body after damage has been done *(like chemotherapy)*.

Protein is an area that all vegan and vegetarian diets struggle with. So if your family practices vegan or vegetarianism, you must be extra vigilant when it comes to sourcing proteins for your child. Think beans, rice, nuts, legumes, and lentils. I recommend animal proteins as your source of protein. Animal proteins have the most complete essential amino acids that your body needs to survive. But if your child was not raised eating meat, they will have trouble processing animal protein. Their body is not use to it. If you do intend on reintroducing animal proteins, do so slowly and with simple animal proteins like white meat chicken, lean pork, or lean seafood.

I also highly recommend combining animal and vegetable protein sources. Examples of this are chicken, beans, and rice; lentils and sausage; fish and rice; chicken and chickpeas; etc. One of my favorite easy to make combos is pitas, grilled chicken, basmati rice, red beans, feta cheese, and a Greek yogurt based sauce.

Fats are used for growth and development. Fat makes up cell membranes. Fat provides cushioning for your organs; helps absorb vitamins A, D, E, and K; and is a great source of energy. Fat molecules contain the most energy of any food source. This is because simple carbohydrates are converted by most living organisms into fat for long term storage. In culinary school, there was an old rule that we add drilled into us over and over again. This was that fat is flavor. We now know, as I have proven in this book, that fat actually isn't flavor. The actual contribution that fat makes to a dish is moistness and energy. Fat also contributes to the feeling of weight in your mouth and stomach. This is why you need to be very careful about the protein sources that you choose. You should stick with lean meats instead of fatty meats. I have paired proteins into the same category because fat is naturally found interspersed inside of muscle tissues. It is also found in other sources of proteins such as nuts, dairy, beans, lentils, and legumes.

One last thing we need to talk about is good fats versus bad fats. Saturated fats and trans fats are generally accepted to increase your risk for heart disease and stroke, as well as gain weight. And let's be honest, we all like to look good! Unsaturated fats are the good kind of fats that are easy to digest and provide great sources of energy. Think avocados, olive oil, and vegetable oils. Don't avoid fats entirely. You need the long term energy in your body. Just simply be aware of the types of fat that you are putting into your child's body.

Carbohydrates

Carbohydrates are macro nutrients that fuel our bodies. They are the most easily and quickly digested form of energy for the human body. They are necessary for function of the central nervous system, kidneys, brain, muscles, and waste elimination. They are mostly found in starchy foods like pasta, rice, barley, oats, wheat, potatoes, and sugar.

The simplest form of a carbohydrate is called glucose. Glucose is the actual chemical that your body burns to fuel itself. When more complicated forms of glucose are introduced, your body will naturally convert them into instant burning fuel or turn them into fats for long term storage. Glucose is commonly known as sugar. This is why when you consume sugary foods and drinks, you get an instant burst of energy and a hard crash later. We want to use carbohydrates in conjunction with fats to provide a smooth burning energy throughout the whole day.

One of the main advantages to eating healthy carbohydrates is that they often come paired with vitamins and minerals that your body needs every day. This makes eating healthy carbohydrates a well rounded choice.

Vitamins and Minerals

Vitamins and minerals are a category of essential nutrients that our body requires to function. These vitamins and minerals are most easily found in fruits and vegetables. But, vitamins and minerals can also be found in most other foods. Vitamins help with the regulation and execution of bodily functions. Where as minerals are used typically to execute a function or build a component. Let's use computers and robots as an example. If your body was a robot, the vitamins would be the pieces of computer software that tell your body how to behave. The minerals would be the nuts and bolts that made up the parts of the robot, as well as specify it's functions and abilities. Two specific vitamins and minerals in action, are vitamin c and calcium. Calcium is used to build bones. Vitamin c regulates immune function. Vitamins and minerals are actually a complicated enough subject to justify writing a book on all their own. Just remember that they are necessary. When we think about vitamins and minerals in meal planning, we are simply thinking of the fruit and vegetable component to our meals.

CHAPTER 6:
MEAL PLANNING

Now that we have the boring nuts and bolts of nutrition out of the way. Let's focus on one of my favorite subjects, which is meal planning. Yay! Insert jazz hands here. Meal planning by definition is exactly what it sounds like. Planning out meals. But where meal planning for me gets really fun, is in the designing of an entire weeks menu.

In this section, I am going to teach you:

1) what are calories,
2) how to make meals that are full of essential nutrients,
3) how to design a menu for the week, and
4) how to grocery shop on a budget

Calories

What are calories? You always hear people talking about calories. Sometimes, they're counting them. Sometimes, they're avoiding them. And other times, they're increasing them. A calorie is not actually something that you can taste, touch, see, or feel. A calorie is not a food item that you eat. It is simply a way of measuring the potential chemical energy contained within a food item. You can use calories to measure the potential energy of pretty much anything including gasoline, kerosene, and anything else combustible. Are you confused yet?

Let me start with the basic scientific definition of a calorie. A calorie is the amount of energy that it takes to raise the temperature of one milliliter of water by one degree Celsius. We use this system of measurement inside of food because when you burn the fats and sugars inside of food, you can actually measure the amount of energy released most easily by using the calorie measurement. Calories are completely independent from the nutrients that we had spoken about earlier. Calories are not protein, fat, carbohydrates, vitamins, or minerals. When we use calories, we simply use them as a way to measure the amount of energy that we are ingesting into our body.

The amount of calories that your body burns can vary wildly. It's determined by a large variety of factors; including how fast your body burns energy naturally, the intensity of physical labor that you do on a daily basis, and a variety of other factors.

To make it simple, there are 3 states that your body exists in:

1) gaining weight, which is a calorie surplus;
2) neither gaining nor loosing weight, which is calorie neutral;
3) loosing weight, which is a calorie deficiency.

Think of your body like a balloon with a slow leak. If we pump more air into the balloon than what escapes through the leak, the balloon will increase in size. If we pump exactly the same amount of air into the balloon as the leak releases, the balloon will maintain the same size. If we pump less air into the balloon than what the leak releases, the balloon will decrease in size. The same is true with human bodies. If you eat too many calories, your body will increase in weight. If you eat to few calories, you will loose weight. If you eat just enough calories, you will maintain your weight. This is important to know because cancer treatment can cause significant weight gain or significant weight loss.

Many kids gain weight during treatment because of the addition of a drug called Prednisone. Prednisone is a commonly prescribed steroid during cancer treatment. It's most common side-effect is to turn cute little children into ravenous beasts who will eat you out of house and home. Because of this hunger, these kids tend to gain a lot of weight during treatment. This is the entire reason we are discussing calories in the first place. It is extremely important to monitor these kids calorie intake so that they do not end up in a state of childhood obesity.

One of the ways that you can combat this ravenous appetite, while reducing calories, is to fill your child's meal with lots of fibrous vegetables. Because fiber cannot be digested, it will sit in your child's stomach, attempting to be processed, and tricking the stomach into thinking it is full for longer. I recommend veggies like carrots and celery. Be warned though there is a very stinky side-effect to increasing fiber. I'll let you draw from that what you will.

Another great technique is to increase lean protein while decreasing carbohydrates. When your body is on steroids, it craves protein to build muscle mass. Carbohydrates are full of calories that will not satisfy your child's food lust. So, try working more lean proteins into their meals and see if that doesn't help.

Just to recap. Remember, calories are simply a way of measuring the potential energy inside of food. The amount of calories in each food item is determined by the food itself. We also want to keep track of calories, especially if your child is gaining or loosing weight. Keeping this information in mind will help us as we move through the meal planning section and allow us to make the best decisions for our child.

How To Make Meals That Are Full Of Essential Nutrients

The heading to this section could honestly be a book in its own right. In fact, I am pretty sure there are several hundred books available on this topic in any given language. I will try to make this as short and sweet as possible and get straight to the point.

Once you begin cooking at home and taking control of your food, making balanced meals is actually surprisingly simple. You want to make sure that your meals contain all of the nutrients that I had spoken about in the nutrition section. So now, let's talk about the quantities that these nutrients should be prepared in.

Here is my formula for success.

25% of the meal should be proteins and fats and 75% should be carbohydrates, vitamins, and minerals.

The average American household simply eats too much meat. A serving of meat is actually 4 ounces. So, a 16 ounce New York strip steak would actually be 4 servings of meat. If you follow the 25-75 rule, you will end up getting more vegetables and carbohydrates naturally into your meals. This technique also naturally makes well rounded meals without even trying. If you do it right, it will even save you money at the grocery store.

Here's a quick example of what a 25-75 meal would look like:

4 ounces of grilled chicken breast (protein)
6 ounces of cauliflower and broccoli mix (vitamins and minerals)
6 ounces of basmati rice (carbohydrates)

Another example of what a 25-75 meal would look like:

4 ounces of grilled chicken breast (protein)
4 ounces of sautéed zucchini (vitamins and minerals)
4 ounces of black beans (carbohydrates)
4 ounces of apple slices (vitamins and minerals)

In this example, the chicken breast is our source of protein. The zucchini and apples make up two different sources in vitamins and minerals. And, we are using the black beans as our source of carbohydrates. While the black beans would normally be considered a protein, in this example, they are functioning more like a carbohydrate than any other nutrient.

The 25-75 rule is a sliding scale. What that means is that you do not have to have exactly proportional amounts of carbohydrates to vitamins and minerals. You can adjust the proportions based on what you are making and on what works best for your body. If you need to increase the protein, you can always increase the protein. But, you want to make sure that you always keep all 3 of those nutrient categories present at the table for every meal. Remember, you are your own best advocate. The same diet does not work for everyone. You need to learn to listen to your body's cravings and understand what it's telling you. For example, I was the guest on a radio show. A very nice woman called in and felt like she was crazy because during breast cancer treatment she craved trout and baked beans. To her, she felt like she was crazy. But that was her body telling her exactly what she needed. I will explain to you here what I explained to her on the radio show.

Trout is a lean and very easily digestible protein source. Because it is a fish, it is also a great source of omega-3, which is a fatty acid. Baked beans are full of protein, carbohydrates, fat, fiber, and other nutrients that your body needs when it is trying to rebuild cells. Remember that very often, cancer treatment involves some form of surgery that your body has to heal after. The best nutrient for that job is protein. So do what works best for your child, and of course work with your dietitians and doctor at the same time.

How To Design A Menu For The Week

Designing a menu is actually really simple once you understand how to do it. Writing a menu is much like creating a successful household budget. You need to take into account every meal and snack that you are going to eat throughout the entire week. The more thorough you are in the designing of the menu, the more successful you will be. To keep this section from getting too long, I am going to teach you the simplified version that I use. This method is the one that I have developed and used. It uses redundant ingredients to help you save money and not waste food. For me, there is no worse feeling than throwing food away that has gone bad from neglect or dis-use.

1) Brainstorm a list of 10 meals that you would like to make for dinner for the week.

10 is not necessarily the rule. What I am trying to convey is that you should brainstorm lots of different ideas so that you can look for opportunities to use common ingredients to help save money and not throw away food. In the beginning, it is a prudent exercise to come up with as many ideas as possible to exercise the newly learned culinary skills that you have acquired from this book. The more you practice, the better and quicker you become at this task.

2) List out underneath each of the meals, the ingredients that it takes to make each of those dishes.

Listing out the ingredients allows you to find the common ingredients and have greater control over your meals. Here, listing out the ingredients also helps you memorize recipes and learn the basic commonalities of different types of dishes.

3) Look for the ingredients that each recipe has in common.

Finding the common ingredients saves you time and money. It allows you to make better decisions before you go to the grocery store.

4) Remove the meals that do not have ingredients in common.

Doing this saves money, time, and your energy. During cancer treatment, using common ingredients makes it easier to prepare your ingredients in advance. This helps make cooking your meals a breeze. For example, if you know that you have 3 recipes that use red onion, you can slice up all the onions you need for the week and place them in a sealed container in the refrigerator to use as you need them. This is a technique that is pulled directly from the restaurant industry. We pre-make, pre-cook, and pre-cut all of the ingredients that go into every appetizer, entrée, or side. We do this because having to cut each ingredient by hand or mix each sauce on the line, as it is ordered, would take too long. Customers would be irate if they had to wait 45 minutes for french toast instead of 10.

5) List out whatever meals you would like for breakfast and their ingredients.

Listing out your meals, makes it easier to pick and choose on the fly. Listing out the ingredients for breakfast allows you to find common ingredients from the dinner menu or breakfast menu.

6) If there are ingredients from the dinner menu that can be used for breakfast or lunch, make certain to purchase sufficient quantities.

Not purchasing a sufficient quantity of an ingredient can be frustrating. This can lead to multiple trips to the grocery store, which is a waste of your valuable time. Make certain to account for every instance and every quantity of ingredient that each recipe calls for.

7) Go out and buy all of the ingredients that are on the grocery list.

Buying all of your ingredients at once saves time and money. When you are acting as a caregiver, there are so many activities that take up your time. Something as simple as going to the grocery store can become a massive chore. Save yourself the headache and get it all done the first time around by creating a grocery list.
This is simply the thought process and methodology that I use when preparing

a menu for the week. Give it a try for a few weeks and then you will be able to develop your own techniques that work best for you and your family.

When we are planning our meals, we need to be calorie conscious and to include of all the nutrients that we talked about in the nutrient section. Choose well rounded meals that include all of the nutrient categories. That is where meal planning and nutrition work hand in hand to make you happy and healthier.

Taking control of your food is taking control of your grocery budget. Taking control of your grocery budget allows you take back control of a part of your life that cancer will normally send into a tail spin. When you are in control, you are empowered to make better and more effective choices in your life. This leads to a better quality of life overall.

How To Grocery Shop On A Budget

Cancer and chemotherapy treatments are expensive! So when you first start seriously cooking at home, one of the hardest things to avoid is spending too much money on food. Here are a few great tips to help minimize your food expense while maximizing impact.

1) Set a realistic monetary food budget and stick to it

This is probably the hardest aspect of staying on target with your money. But, it's amazing how if you work inside your food budget, how your meals will change in quality and character very quickly. Setting a food budget helps you control your food cost and forces you to learn how much each item costs. This makes it easier to make budget minded decisions while making your menu. The best way to help you stick to your budget is to keep track of how much you are spending while you are shopping. This will help keep you accountable and help you to learn how much your food actually costs.

2) Plan a menu for the week

When you plan a menu, not only do you have a road map of what you are going to create but it allows you to cook similarly themed food items which reduces the need to purchase a lot of unique ingredients. For example, let's say you have a recipe that requires carrots, onions, and celery. This mixture, typically known as mirepoix, forms the backbone of almost every classic western culinary recipe. Just by using the mirepoix mixture, we can make recipes like soup, pot roast, and Shepard's pie. The variations are endless. Carrots, onions, and celery are budget friendly. They also last a long time in the refrigerator and are full of healthy fiber. So as you can see, using similarly themed ingredients can help you save money on a budget.

3) Don't impulse purchase

One of the biggest expenses you will run into when buying food at the grocery store is the impulse purchase. I myself am extremely guilty of perusing the cheese area and selecting a few things that topple the food budget right over. That's why I always send my wife with the exact list of what I need. She won't come back with extra things like a super rare piece of cheese that I absolutely had to try! Another thing that will make you impulse on food at the grocery store is if you go shopping when you are hungry. Don't buy food when you are hungry. Eat first, then shop!

4) Prep and freeze perishable food items

Aside from impulse purchasing, food waste is the biggest way to blow your grocery budget! If you are throwing away $20 worth of food every week, that's $20 of loss on your grocery budget. That money could have been better spent in other categories of your life. What we do in our home, is take perishable food items, like fresh veggies, pre-slice them, place them into freezer bags, and simply freeze them for later use. $20 a week adds up to $1040 per year. That can buy a lot of other fun stuff like vacations, movie tickets, and video games. Don't let that much money end up in the trash.

5) Use your leftovers to make other recipes

A great thing about leftovers is that you can turn them into other recipes. For example, pot roast can be made into beef stew. Roasted chicken breast can be turned into chicken noodle soup. I like to play a game that I call "The Leftovers Game." This is where I try to re-create a recipe of some kind while incorporating leftovers from a completely different recipe. The trick to this is proper seasoning and of course incorporating new and fresh food ingredients as well.

6) Eat your leftovers

In our house, leftovers translates to one word: lunch. We eat our leftovers for lunch throughout the week. My wife can eat leftovers the next day. I, on the other hand, usually need to wait a few days. Leftovers, if properly stored and sealed, usually stay fresh for about a week in the refrigerator and longer in the freezer.

7) Organic ingredients are expensive

Organic ingredients are significantly more expensive than their regular everyday counterparts. If you want to eat organic, by all means just go ahead and do it. But, you don't have to feel guilty if you don't. As a parent, your drive is to give your children the greatest opportunities that you can present them; including food, schooling, and homes. But feeding your kids organic food is not a stamp of quality parenting. What makes something "organic" is incredibly misunderstood. What gives you the quality stamp of "parent of the year" is by making a conscious effort to make healthier choices in the meals that you are providing your children.

Organic ingredients have absolutely no measurable additional nutritional, health, or flavor benefits. An apple, whether organic or conventional, will still have the same nutrients. There are far greater measurable variances based on location grown, type of soil, sun exposure, and many other numerous factors. Because organic ingredients are not treated using modern preservation techniques, they also spoil faster. The best way to get organic food on your table is to grow it yourself. Then, you are getting the freshest ingredients possible on your table.

One of the main reasons that people advocate for the use of organic ingredients is because they claim that organic farmers do not use herbicides or pesticides. That is simply not true. Organic farmers use pesticides on their foods just like conventional farmers do. The only way to guarantee that there are no herbicides or pesticides in your food is to grow your own food and not use herbicides or pesticides.

More on "Going Organic"

Organic ingredients tend to be 3-4 times as expensive as their average everyday counterparts. "Going organic" is not what improves your health or well being. What improves your health or well being is the conscious decision to eat healthier and more complete meals.

The best story I've ever heard about the misunderstanding around organic ingredients came from a friend of mine who is a dietitian. She told me about a patient of hers who kept eating cookies when they were not suppose to be. My friend confronted the patient about why they continued to eat so many cookies. The patient justified themselves by explaining that the cookies were organic and therefore healthy for them.

We both laughed for a good long while about that story. But, I am using it today to explain that an organic cookie has the same calories and nutritional benefits of a regular cookie. They are in no way actually different. Purchasing organic arose out of a fear of the unknown. The unknown was about herbicides and pesticides being used in the modern production of food. Simply make better and healthier decisions like choosing an orange for a snack instead of a cookie. And, you will be just fine.

For further reading on organic vs. conventional, I am providing the following online sources so that you are completely and totally informed beyond the scope of this work.

Scientific American
http://blogs.scientificamerican.com/science-sushi/httpblogsscientificamerican comscience-sushi20110718mythbusting-101-organic-farming-conventional-agriculture/

Harvard Health Publications
http://www.health.harvard.edu/blog/organic-food-no-more-nutritious-than-conventionally-grown-food-201209055264

Science Direct -Organic food and the impact on human health
http://www.sciencedirect.com/science/article/pii/S1573521411000054

American Journal of Clinical Nutrition -Nutritional quality of organic foods: a systematic review
http://m.ajcn.nutrition.org/content/early/2009/07/29/ajcn.2009.28041.abstract

Medicine Net
http://www.medicinenet.com/script/main/mobileart.asp?articlekey=104207

Mayo Clinic
http://www.mayoclinic.org/healthy-lifestyle/nutrition-and-healthy-eating/in-depth/organic-food/art-20043880?pg=2

Armed with this new knowledge, I am very confident that you will all be able to make better decisions, save money, plan meals, and adjust your calories as appropriate. Remember, cooking is an art that you develop and so are the skills that surround meal planning.

Now, we will move into the recipes section where can begin to practice everything you just learned.

CHAPTER 7:
PRACTICE RECIPES

Explanation For The Practice Recipes

Welcome to the Practice Recipes section! As I had stated in the forward to this book, this is not a cookbook in the traditional sense that you are buying it for the recipes. You bought this book to learn how-to adjust your cooking for eating related side-effects from cancer treatment. I have provided these recipes as foundations of learning so that you may practice your new found skills in a fun, practical, and easy fashion.

These recipes were taken from my first book, *Cooking for Chemo ...and After!* These practice recipes are provided as a way to refine and hone your new cooking skills in the same way that a mathematics textbook will have math problems for you to solve. The problems in a math book may not be the actual ones that you need to solve in real life, but they equip you with the knowledge to solve other math problems in the future. It is with this spirit in mind that I provide these recipes for you to practice. You will be able to take your new cooking knowledge and practice it on the recipes in this book. Then you will be able take your knowledge and experience, and begin to apply it to new recipes that are not in this book. This gives you the opportunity to understand and adjust flavor in your everyday life. It also helps to achieve one of my goals from *Cooking for Chemo ...and After!* which is to build an army of chefs to change the world.

Let's not beat around the bush. Kids are picky! I could provide 10,000 recipes and your kid could still hate every last one of them. Nobody knows your child better than you do. So, I am entrusting you with the responsibility of cooking foods for your child that they like, love, and enjoy.

You will notice that these recipes are laid out VERY differently than the recipes in other books. I have done this so that you can begin to understand the purpose of each component inside of a recipe.

There are five categories that this section is divided into:

Big Meals
Sides
Sauces
Soups
Smoothies

Each food subject has supplemental information at the beginning of each section. This is to help further your knowledge and to give you any additional quick tips or general information you may need.

Remember to use what you have learned. Adjust the recipes for the flavor profile of the child you are cooking for and allow for their specific taste changes. So, if that calls for an omission of certain ingredients from a recipe and the addition of others; then I hereby charge, grant, and empower you with full rights, power, and responsibility to do so.

If and when you do make substitutes, make sure it is an equal substitution. For example, protein for protein or vegetable for vegetable. Remember to substitute like for like. A good example is if something calls for carrots, but you don't like carrots or can no longer eat them. Substitute the carrots for a different kind of vegetable that you can eat, like corn or green beans. A specific example of substitutions in my life is when I made chili using chicken breast, pork chops, and baked beans instead of the traditional chili beans and ground beef. In conclusion, don't be afraid to substitute or play around with these recipes as you see fit or require.

Please Note On These Recipes:

Seasoning amounts are subjective. Remember not to over-season and to taste your food as you go. Do not take all recipes as literal truth of measurement but as an idea of where to start. The purpose of these recipes is to capture the essence of the dish. In doing this, I have provided these general recipe guidelines as minimum estimates of ingredients you should have on-hand to complete the recipe. You do not need to put the full amount called for into the recipe. This is simply how much to allow for. It is not an exact called for scientific measurement. Again, this is because everyone's taste changes are a little different.

You have to learn how to adjust the seasonings to cater to your child's specific changes. For example, my chicken and dumplings recipe calls for ½ tsp cayenne pepper. Most people find this to be way too spicy. But, there are a select group of people that need all their recipes extra spicy. This is why I have called for a ½ tsp. Most children have not been exposed to spicy on a regular basis. As a result, they are spicy sensitive. So in this example, I would not put the entire ½ tsp of cayenne pepper into the recipe. I would instead put a pinch of cayenne pepper or just omit it entirely.

If you follow this advice, you will automatically save yourself the trouble of fixing something that never needed to be broken. Cooking is a creative art. Don't be afraid to create. Don't be afraid to adjust.

Last but not least, the recipes are laid out in the following format for educational purposes and for ease of use. I feel that it is extremely important to carry over what I just taught you and lay it out in an easy to use way that helps you practice what you just learned. As all of us caregivers know, time is of the essence! The ability to learn and adapt quickly makes all the difference when feeding children undergoing cancer treatments.

Practice Recipe Layout

Name of Recipe
At the top of each page you will see the recipe name. This is what the dish is called.

Ease of Preparation/Level
I decided to label each dish according to it's ease of preparation. While most dishes in this book are a Level 1 *(beginner level)*, I don't want someone who has never cooked attempting a Level 3 *(advanced level)* dish. It might not turn out right and I don't want you to get frustrated and quit. This book is here to help you begin learning and adapting at the experience level you are currently at.

Recipes range from Level 1 to Level 3. Level 1 is a dish that any beginner can make. Level 2 is a dish that may require a little more cooking experience in order for it to turn out correctly. Level 3 is for those who are more advanced in cooking. This cookbook has a ton of Level 1 recipes so don't get discouraged if you are new to cooking! After enough practice, you will have the confidence to move to the next level. Advanced cooks: You should be able to fine tune your skills and quickly catch on to what I am teaching you.

Recipe Description
This is a description of the recipe you are about to make. I did this to help give you a better idea and understanding of the big picture of what you are about to cook. I also used this to throw in some fun facts about different foods and their origins.

Tasting Guidelines
This is probably the single most important section of each recipe. This is the part that teaches you how to think like a chef. It gives you a set of guidelines that allows you to consider the recipe as a conceptual idea. Then, you can store this information in your mind and reference your knowledge when your child asks for something specific or has new side-effects to compensate for. Think of these like search keywords. What am I searching for? Is it savory, soft, fun, easy? This is the purpose of the Tasting Guidelines.

Ingredients

This is where the ingredients, their amounts, and how they need to be prepared will be listed.

Flavor Balancers

This is where the seasonings and their amounts, as required by the recipe, will be listed.

Aromatics

This is where the herbs and spices *(aromatics)* that are not listed in the Flavor Balancers section will be. I separated aromatics because I want you to physically see and begin to understand what gives your food its' nose and that extra UMPH!

Recipe Directions

This is how to make the recipe. Remember to fully read through all the information listed for the recipe ahead of time. That will prevent you from making big mistakes when you get to this section and begin making the recipe.

Chef Tips

This is where you find extra information and pro tips that will help further your knowledge and understanding of why certain things are done the way they are when you are making the recipes. Make sure to read the chef tips before starting any recipe.

With all of that said and done, let's get started!

BIG MEALS

Beef Shepherd's Pie

Ease of Preparation
Level 2-Intermediate

Recipe Description
Beef shepherd's pie is a classic dish from the British Isles. Typically made with lamb, we have substituted with lean ground beef for ease of preparation, weight, and flavor palate. Lamb is fatty and heavy, making it a poor choice during cancer treatments. This dish is a layered casserole with a beef, vegetable, and gravy mixture comprising the filling with mashed potatoes layered on top, which acts as the pie crust.

Tasting Guidelines
Taste is **savory** and hearty.
Weight is **heavy** but can be balanced with vinegar.
Texture is **soft.**
For **low to moderate** side effects.
Emotional response of **warm lovey goodness.**
Best categorized as a **comfort food.**

Ingredients
1 lb. lean ground beef
1 lb. frozen veggie mix *(a 4-in-1 mix, small diced veggies)*
2 packs brown gravy mix prepared according to directions
1 tbsp. cooking oil
mashed potatoes *(prepared according to the recipe in this book)*

Flavor Balancers
1/2 tbsp. black pepper
1 tbsp. red wine vinegar
1 tbsp. sugar

Aromatics
1 tbsp. garlic, minced

Recipe Directions

Preheat oven to 425°F. In a large but high-sided sauté pan, bring oil to medium heat. Add ground beef and garlic together. Cook ground beef, constantly chopping it to make small pieces. Add black pepper to taste. After beef has been sufficiently browned, add veggies and a quarter cup of water. Increase heat to medium-high, allowing vegetables to steam lightly while stirring constantly. When veggies are thoroughly warmed, add brown gravy, mixing thoroughly. The key here is to have gravy coating everything but to not have the food swimming in the gravy.

Pick a suitable casserole dish made out of either glass or ceramic (ceramic seems to taste better for some reason), depending on how you like your shepherd's pie. You can choose the depth of the dish. So for example, if you prefer an equal mixture of potatoes and filling, use a larger, shallower dish. If you prefer more filling to potato, use a smaller, deeper dish.

Chef Tips

Get a large icing bag. If you do not have one, you can make one out of a one-gallon Ziploc bag by cutting a quarter inch off one of the bottom corners. Fill the bag with potatoes that are warm but not scalding hot. And pipe like frosting, in a snake-like motion, back and forth, over the entirety of dish until all corners are covered. Fill bag with potatoes as necessary. Lightly spray potatoes with cooking spray and place in oven until potatoes are thoroughly toasted. You will know at this point whether you mixed the gravy at the proper proportion or not. If gravy rises up and bubbles though the potatoes, and forms lakes of gravy, you have put too much gravy in there. If lakes of gravy do not form, then you have put the proper amount of gravy in.

Beef Stroganoff

Ease of Preparation
Level 1-Easy

Recipe Description

A hearty egg noodle and gravy dish. Very easy to prepare and an infinite amount of variations. Odds are you have had this at some point in your life, whether in a school cafeteria, a TV dinner, or a high-end restaurant.

Tasting Guidelines

Taste is rich and **savory.**
Weight is **heavy** but can be balanced with vinegar.
Texture is **soft.**
For **low to moderate** treatment side effect.
Emotional response of a **good home cooked meal.**
Best categorized as **classic Russian.**

Ingredients

8–16 oz. of beef for stew
1/4 c. whole milk
1 package of egg noodles, cooked and lightly oiled, set to side
1 yellow onion, medium diced
1 small pack Portabella mushrooms, chopped
8 oz. sour cream
8 oz butter *(2 Sticks)*
1 can cream of mushroom soup
2 packages brown gravy prepared according to mix directions

Flavor Balancers

1 cup red wine
1 tbsp. black pepper
2 tbsp. red wine vinegar
1 tbsp. sugar

Aromatics

1/2 tbsp. rosemary
2 tbsp. flat leaf Italian parsley, chopped

Recipe Directions

Take beef and tenderize with a meat mallet. Place tenderized beef into a mixing bowl. Salt and pepper beef pieces on both sides to taste. Allow to marinate 30 minutes on the counter.

In a large sauté pan, melt butter over medium heat. Sweat onion and mushrooms in butter until onions are translucent. Add beef, rosemary, black pepper, red wine, red wine vinegar, and sugar. Cook beef until thoroughly cooked through. When beef is thoroughly cooked, stir in brown gravy, cream of mushroom soup, and sour cream. Mix well. Allow to simmer on low heat uncovered for 10 minutes. If sauce is too thick add milk to thin. Serve over egg noodles. Top with Italian flat leaf parsley and enjoy.

Chef Tips

This is a really great recipe. It reheats well. If the recipe is a little too heavy, add a little extra red wine vinegar or lemon juice to cut through the weight of the dish.

Chicken and Broccoli Cheese Casserole

Ease of Preparation
Level 1-Easy

Recipe Description
Chicken and broccoli cheese casserole is a classic, go-to dish when you don't have the time to do anything but throw dinner in the oven and hope for the best.

Tasting Guidelines
Taste is cheesy and **savory.**
Weight is **medium** but can be balanced with vinegar and sugar.
Texture is soft.
For **low to moderate** side effects.
Emotional response of **home cooked love.**
Best categorized as a **comfort food.**

Ingredients
1 lb. chicken breast, cooked and cut into quarter inch cubes
8 oz. sharp cheddar cheese, shredded
2 c. white rice, cooked
1 package frozen broccoli, chopped
1 small yellow onion, chopped
1 can cream mushroom
1 can broccoli cheese soup *(Campbell's)*

Flavor Balancers
kosher salt to taste
1 tbsp. soy sauce
black pepper to taste
1 tbsp. red wine vinegar
1 tbsp. sugar

Garnish
French's cheddar flavored fried french onions

Recipe Directions

Preheat the oven to 425°F. Combine all ingredients in a large mixing bowl, except for the french onion crisps. After thoroughly mixed, check for consistency. If soup doesn't cover all ingredients thoroughly, add a little bit of milk until mixture is homogenous. Transfer to a large casserole dish. Pack mixture down into all corners. Cover with french onion crisps and allow to bake uncovered until internal temperature reaches 145°F.

Chef Tips

My mom absolutely loved this dish! And it is super tasty for breakfast, lunch, or dinner. It's full of fat, protein, and carbohydrates, but is also very easy to digest. This is good for people with mouth sores because it is very soft and if you mix the french onions into the casserole after baked but before serving they loose their crunchiness but maintain a strong pop of flavor. A tablespoon of red wine vinegar will lighten the dish. A couple shakes of red pepper will fill the dish. And would highly recommend NOT adding to much extra sugar as the rice will break down in the casserole naturally imparting sugar. For a more aromatic quality, add some sage and thyme.

Chicken Cacciatore

Recipe Description

A classic Italian dish. Fairly popular in Italian restaurants until recently when it was disregarded and categorized as old fashioned. It is characterized by chicken breasts covered in tomatoes and veggies then baked in the oven until it is fork tender.

Tasting Guidelines

Taste is **savory, sweet,** and a touch of **spicy.**
Weight is **light** but can be balanced with savory and sugar.
Texture is **soft.**
For **low to moderate** treatment side effects.
Emotional response of **home cooked Italian goodness.**
Best categorized as **family style Italian fare.**

Ingredients

3 lbs. chicken breast, uncooked and cut into bite-sized pieces
1 large can tomatoes, diced
4 stalks celery, chopped
4 carrots, chopped
1 yellow onion, diced
8 oz. portabella mushrooms, sliced
1 can corn kernels, drained
1 c. peas *(Snow peas if you can get them. Frozen peas work, too.)*
2 tbsp. olive oil

Flavor Balancers

1/2 tbsp. salt
1 c. red wine
1/2 tbsp. black pepper
3 shakes red pepper flakes
2 tbsp. red wine vinegar
1/4 cup sugar

Aromatics

1 bay leaf
1 tbsp. rosemary
½ tbsp. dried oregano
1 tsp. fennel seed
1 fennel bulb, sliced into medium strips, (*optional*)
1 zucchini, unpeeled and quartered

Recipe Directions

Mix all ingredients together in a large mixing bowl. Preheat oven to 375°F. Pour ingredients into large casserole dish. (*Several dishes may be required.*) Bake uncovered for about an hour and a half or until sauce naturally thickens. Serve with a side of basmati rice or angel hair pasta tossed in olive oil, pepper, and Parmesan.

Chef Tips

The beauty of this dish is that there is no wrong way to make it. The origin of this dish comes from the Italian "Pollo Alla Cacciatore," which means chicken prepared in the style of a hunter. Simplified, we call this Hunters-style chicken. The intended expression of this dish is that you would throw whatever you had available, be it wild mushrooms, celery, carrots, or whatever else you could find in nature and cook it all together. Originally this would have been prepared with a whole chicken roasted over an open fire perhaps using a dutch oven or using some other similar camping style cookware. So when you prepare this dish, feel free to use whatever veggies you have available on hand, and don't worry about using the exact ingredients for accuracy.

Chicken Pot Pie Casserole

Ease of Preparation
Level 1-Easy

Recipe Description

This recipe is for what I consider to be the easiest way to make a chicken pot pie. The biscuit dough on top adds a nice deviation from the standard flavorless pie crust and makes it fun to eat. The best thing about this dish is it tastes even better as leftovers.

Tasting Guidelines

Taste is **savory** and hearty.
Weight is **medium-heavy** but can be balanced with savory, vinegar, and sugar.
Texture is **soft.**
For **low to moderate** treatment side effects.
Emotional response of a **dinner your mom would have made.**
Best categorized as **classic American.**

Ingredients

3 chicken breasts, cooked and chopped
1/2 c. of cheddar cheese
6 oz. red potatoes, medium diced
6 oz. carrots, medium diced
1 yellow onion, medium diced
6 oz. peas
6 oz. corn kernels
1 can cream of chicken
1 can cream of mushroom
1–2 cups of water
2 tbsp. olive oil
Your favorite baking quick mix prepared for biscuits but adding 1 tsp. baking soda

Flavor Balancers

kosher salt to taste
2 tbsp. soy sauce
black pepper to taste
2 tbsp. apple cider vinegar or red wine vinegar
2 tbsp. sugar *(if using red wine vinegar)*

Aromatics

2 teaspoons red curry powder
1 tbsp. ground sage

Recipe Directions

Cook your chicken breast. I personally like to use the quick frozen ones for convenience. And to cook them, I will boil them in water until thoroughly cooked. While this is going, sauté your veggies in olive oil together. Be careful not to burn them. Add chopped chicken. Sauté until chicken gets a light brown color.

Prepare your biscuit dough as directed, making certain to add the baking soda. Once chicken has gotten a little golden brown on it. Add your spices and seasonings except for soy sauce, vinegar, and sugar. After mixing seasonings thoroughly, add the soy sauce and coat all food thoroughly. Allow soy sauce to reduce. Add vinegar allow to reduce. Add sugar and canned soups. Mix well. If needed, add water to adjust thickness. Add cheddar cheese mixing thoroughly. Pour filling mixture into a large casserole dish, preferably glass or ceramic dish.

At this point, it is all personal preference.

Method 1

Roll out biscuit dough into a long sheet of dough. Place sheet of dough over filling, making certain that the dough is larger than the casserole dish. Cut off excess trimmings. Cut small cuts in dough to allow pot pie to vent while cooking.

Method 2

The "drop biscuit" method. This is my preferred method because I feel that it adds a certain Southern charm to it. You take the biscuit dough and either roll out the dough onto a sheet and cut biscuits, laying the biscuits on top of the filling. Or free form balls of dough with your hands, about the size of a golf ball, and dot the top of the pot pie filling with freshly made drop biscuit dough.
Bake in preheated oven at 375°F until biscuits/pie covering is thoroughly cooked, about 15 minutes.

Chef Tips

If you are in a hurry and time is of the essence, feel free to save some time and pick up pre-made biscuit dough from your grocery store.

Chicken Shepherd's Pie

Ease of Preparation
Level 2-Intermediate

Recipe Description
Chicken shepherd's pie is my personal take on the classic dish. It's very similar in construction to the classic shepherd's pie, but it uses chicken in a cream sauce instead of ground beef in a brown gravy. You get the same comforting notes that you get with a regular shepherd's pie but with a twist.

Tasting Guidelines
Taste is **savory** with aromatic herb notes.
Weight is **medium** but can be balanced with spicy and savory.
Texture is **soft.**
For **low to moderate** treatment side effects.
Emotional response of a **good home cooked meal.**
Best categorized as a **comfort food.**

Ingredients
1 lb. chicken breast, cooked and cut into 1/2" cubes
1 c. sharp cheddar cheese, shredded *(or Swiss)*
1 lb. frozen veggie mix *(something like a 4-in-1, it needs to be small diced veggies)*
1 small can cream mushroom soup
1 small can cream chicken soup
1 tbsp. cooking oil
mashed potatoes (prepared according to the recipe in this book)

Flavor Balancers
1/2½ tbsp. black pepper
1 tbsp. red wine vinegar
1/2 tbsp. sugar

Aromatics
1 tbsp. garlic, minced
1 tsp. rosemary
1 tsp. thyme
1 tsp. sage, ground

Recipe Directions

Preheat oven to 425°F. In a large but high-sided sauté pan, bring oil to medium heat. Add cubed chicken breast and garlic together. Cook until chicken develops a little browning on all sides. Add black pepper to taste. After chicken has been sufficiently browned, add veggies and a quarter cup of water increase heat to medium-high, allowing vegetables to steam lightly while stirring constantly. When veggies are thoroughly warmed, add canned soups, cheese, and remaining seasonings, mixing thoroughly. The key here is to have gravy coating everything but to not have the food swimming in the gravy.

Chef Tips

Pick a suitable casserole dish made out of either glass or ceramic, depending on how you like your shepherd's pie. You can choose the depth of the dish. So for example, if you prefer an equal mixture of potatoes and filling, use a larger, shallower dish. If you prefer more filling to potato, use a smaller, deeper dish.

Get a large icing bag. If you do not have one, you can make one out of a one-gallon Ziploc bag by cutting a quarter inch off one of the bottom corners. Fill the bag with potatoes that are warm but not scalding hot. And pipe like frosting, in a snake-like motion, back and forth, over the entirety of dish until all corners are covered. Fill bag with potatoes as necessary. Lightly spray potatoes with cooking spray and place in oven until potatoes are thoroughly toasted. You will know at this point whether you mixed the gravy at the proper proportion or not. If gravy rises up and bubbles though the potatoes, and forms lakes of gravy, you have put too much gravy in there. If lakes of gravy do not form, then you have put the proper amount of gravy in.

Chicken Tetrazzini

Ease of Preparation
Level 1-Easy

Recipe Description
A delicious if unauthentic American-Italian dish. The highlight of this dish is the excessive use of Parmesan and the unashamed use of a generous cream sauce. This dish is another one of my family's favorite recipes. It was first brought into our family by my grandparents neighborhood gourmet club.

Tasting Guidelines
Taste is cheesy, creamy, and **savory.**
Weight is **heavy** but can be balanced with lemon juice or vinegar.
Texture is **soft.**
For **low** treatment side effects.
Emotional response of being **warm and loved.**
Best categorized as **American-Italian.**

Ingredients
4 chicken breast, seasoned with salt and pepper, grilled, and cut into cubes
2 c. Parmesan cheese, grated
1 lb. linguine noodles
1 medium yellow onion, diced
8 oz. Portabella mushrooms, sliced
1 small jar pimentos
1 c. heavy whipping cream
2 ounces butter (½ stick)
4 tbsp. flour

Flavor Balancers
1 tbsp. soy sauce
1 tbsp. black pepper
1 tbsp. red wine vinegar
2 tbsp. sugar

Aromatics
2 tbsp. garlic, minced
1 tbsp. dried oregano

Recipe Directions

Prepare sauce. Melt butter over medium heat in large sauté pan. Add mushrooms, onions, and garlic. Sauté until onions and mushrooms sweat and onions are translucent. Add soy sauce, pepper, red wine vinegar, and sugar. Stir in flour to soak up the excess butter. Whisk in cream. Allow to thicken. Remove from heat. Stir in pimentos and half of the Parmesan.

In a large mixing bowl, combine cooked noodles, sauce, and chicken, stirring thoroughly. Transfer to a large casserole dish. Cover top with Parmesan. Bake together in a 350°F oven until Parmesan is golden brown across the top.

Chef Tips

If it doesn't look like there is going to be enough sauce, add milk to stretch sauce out. This is a family recipe so my mom was extremely partial to this recipe.

Grilled Cheese and Tomato Soup

Recipe Description

An American dinner classic. Perfectly grilled bread with slices of American cheese. Served with hot tomato soup. This is my wife's favorite when she is feeling sick or sad.

Tasting Guidelines

Taste is **savory and salty.**
Weight is **light.**
Texture is **crunchy sandwich** with **soft soup.**
For people with **low to severe** side effects.
Emotional response of **pure love** when you sick or sad.
Best categorized as **classic home-style American.**

Ingredients

2 slices bread
2 slices American cheese *(processed American cheddar cheese slices)*
1 can condensed tomato soup, small
8 oz. whole milk
butter or margarine

Flavor Balancers

kosher salt to taste
black pepper to taste, ground
1 tsp red wine vinegar
1 tsp sugar

Recipe Directions
Grilled Cheese

Spread butter or margarine thinly over one-side of each slice of bread. Very lightly sprinkle less than a pinch of salt evenly on top of the butter. Pre-heat griddle or large sauté pan to a medium heat. Place butter side of bread onto heat. Immediately place American cheese slices on top of each piece of bread. Grill bread until bread has a medium toast. Not too dark. Not too light. You want a nice golden brown color. Remove slices of bread from heat. Press each piece of toasted sliced bread together ensuring that the cheese is on the inside. Allow to rest 30 seconds before slicing sandwich diagonally.

Tomato Soup

Place a medium sized sauce pan over medium heat. Add contents of soup can, milk, red wine vinegar, and sugar. Whisk together over medium heat until soup begins to simmer. When soup begins to simmer, add black pepper to taste if desired. Remove from heat and serve soup hot.

Chef Tips
Grilled Cheese Sandwich

What is American cheese? American cheese is a food product from the turn of the 20th century that was simply a way to preserve cheddar cheese for a longer time. Especially given the harsh conditions that Americans lived in during that time. The real name of this cheese is processed American cheddar cheese. In the United States, we simply call it "American cheese" as a shortened version of the long name. The processing of the American cheddar cheese makes the cheddar cheese softer, saltier, and melt when exposed to heat. This makes it an ideal cheese for situations where a rich, nutty cheese flavor is required for heat applications. Standard cheddar does not melt the same way that American cheese does and will instead simply become greasy when you apply heat to it. You can substitute any cheese that melts well. For example, Gruyère or Gouda make an excellent substitution for the American cheese. If you cannot find American cheese due to your region, an equally appropriate substitute would be a sharp English cheddar.

I put salt on the butter side of the bread because the salt enhances and complements the flavor of the American cheese.

Tomato Soup

Do not allow soup to boil or burn as either of these will completely ruin the soup. I personally like to put a light finely ground black pepper in my grilled cheese sandwiches as well. I would advise you to do the same. The key to this dish is taking your time and going slowly so you don't burn anything.

Lasagna, Baked

Recipe Description
A classic Italian dish famous the world over for its layered pasta with delicious filling.

Tasting Guidelines
Taste is **savory,** cheesy, and meaty.

Weight is **heavy** but can be balanced with vinegar and sugar.

Texture is **soft.**

For **low to moderate** treatment side effects.

Emotional response of **home cooked goodness.**

Best categorized as classic **Italian.**

Ingredients
1 lb. ground Italian sausage, cooked and browned *(like prepared for tacos)*

1 lb. lean ground beef, cooked and browned *(like prepared for tacos)*

16 oz. mozzarella cheese, shredded

16 oz. ricotta cheese

8 oz. feta cheese

2 oz. Parmesan cheese, grated

1 box lasagna noodles

1 batch of marinara *(follow recipe in this book)*

1 green bell pepper, chopped

1 red bell pepper, chopped

1 lb. fresh spinach

1 c. olive oil

Flavor Balancers
1 tbsp. black pepper

1 tbsp. lemon juice

1 tbsp. sugar

Aromatics
2 tbsp. garlic, minced

1 tbsp. fresh Italian flat leaf parsley, chopped

Recipe Directions

Prepare lasagna noodles as directed in well-salted water. *(Water should taste like the ocean.)* Drain noodles. Spray noodles down with cold water to stop the cooking process. Cover well with olive oil. Transfer to container and set to the side.

Ricotta, Feta, Spinach Filling

In a large sauté pan over medium heat, sauté garlic and the red and green peppers until garlic is light brown. Immediately, add fresh spinach and using a flipping/folding method wilt the spinach. As soon as spinach is wilted, remove from heat and pour into a mixing bowl. Add ricotta, feta, black pepper, salt, sugar, vinegar, lemon juice, and parsley into mixing bowl. Using a large spoon, mix and mash all ingredients together until all ingredients are blended together well. Set mixture to side.

Assembly

Grease a large casserole pan with olive oil. Place a thin layer of marinara on the bottom of the pan followed by one layer of lasagna noodles. Spread a thin layer of the ricotta mixture on top of the noodles, taking care not to rip them. Place another layer of lasagna noodles on top. Apply a thin layer of marinara and sprinkle ground beef and sausage. Repeat this layering technique until there are no more noodles left, making certain to use all ingredients and to do each layer fairly evenly. The thickness of your layers is determined by the size of your pan. So adjust as you go, using best judgment.

When you reach your final top layer of noodles, cover with a healthy layer of marinara, making certain to not leave any dry spots what so ever and getting it down into the edges as well. Cover the marinara with a healthy sprinkling of mozzarella and Parmesan cheese.

Place assembled lasagna in oven and bake at 325°F about 2 hours or until center has reach 145°F. If the center of the lasagna reaches 145°F before the cheese starts to brown, simply turn on the broiler and broil on low to finish taking care not to burn. When done baking, top with fresh Italian parsley.

Linguine with Peperonata

Ease of Preparation
Level 2-Intermediate

Recipe Description

A surprisingly light pasta dish. Fabulous for summers on the back porch. This dish is characterized by its peppers and sausage and goes especially well with a glass of Chianti.

Tasting Guidelines

Taste is **savory** and sweet.
Weight is **light** but can be balanced with vinegar and red wine.
Texture is **soft.**
For **low to moderate** treatment side effects.
Emotional response of sitting on the Italian riviera enjoying a **good meal** and a glass of wine.
Best categorized as **Italian.**

Ingredients

1 lb. linguine noodles
1 c. peperonata, *(follow recipe in this book)*
1 c. marinara, *(follow recipe in this book)*
1/4 lb. Italian sausage
1/4 cup red wine, for deglazing pan

Recipe Directions

Prepare peperonata and marinara according to their recipes in this book. In a large pan, brown the sausage on medium-high heat, taking care to drain excess grease. After sausage has been drained, mix in pereronata and bring to temperature. Add red wine to deglaze pan. After red wine begins to reduce, stir in marinara and reduce to a medium-low heat. Allow marinara to come to proper temperature with out burning it.

Boil linguine noodles in water that is as salty as the ocean. When done, drain noodles well. Toss in sauce, coating evenly. Serve with crusty bread, Parmesan, or riccotta salata.

Chef Tips

Make sure that you drain the sausage grease well. The dish is supposed to be light in weight and flavor. If you do not have previously made peperonata, you can make in the same pan as the sausage, after the sausage has been browned and drained of excess grease.

Mac 'n' Cheese, Baked

Ease of Preparation
Level 1-Easy

Recipe Description
A classic casserole dish from the 1950s. This dish is characterized by it's ease of preparation and savory, cheesy flavor.

Tasting Guidelines
Taste is **savory** and cheesy with a hint of salty.
Weight is **heavy** but can be balanced with vinegar.
Texture is **soft.**
For people with **low to moderate** treatment side effects.
Emotional response of **fun childhood memories.**
Best categorized as **comfort food.**

Ingredients
4 slices American bacon, chopped and cooked crispy
1 lb. elbow macaroni, cooked in salted water
8 oz. sharp cheddar, shredded
8 oz. American cheddar, shredded
1/2 yellow onion, chopped
1 c. milk
1 tbsp. butter
1 tbsp. flour

Flavor Balancers
1 tsp. kosher salt
1/2 tbsp. black pepper
1 tsp. red pepper flakes
1 tbsp. red wine vinegar
1/2 tbsp. sugar

Aromatics
1 tbsp. garlic, minced
1 tbsp. Old Bay seasoning

Recipe Directions

Preheat your oven to 375°F . In a large sauce pan, melt butter over medium heat. Add onion and garlic. Allow onions to caramelize stirring frequently. Stir in flour until butter is absorbed. Add milk. Stir thoroughly, avoiding burning the milk. Add seasonings and cheese. Mix thoroughly and taste for flavor. Slowly stir in macaroni. If there is not enough sauce, slowly add milk until pasta is thoroughly coated. Adjust seasonings as necessary and stir in cooked bacon. Bake in deep casserole dish at least 15 minutes.

Chef Tips

To make this more of a meal, add some cooked, cubed chicken breast. This is a fantastic meal in itself or used as a side. You could also serve this mac and cheese as soon as it's prepared to save yourself the time of baking. The advantage to baking is that it gives the flavors time to melt together. You also get nice crispy edges.

Mostaccioli, Baked

Recipe Description

Baked mostaccioli is a native dish to St. Louis, Missouri. It is our version of Chicago's baked ziti except we use mostaccioli or penne noodles instead, giving the dish a completely different texture. In this dish, pasta is tossed in the sauce, covered with cheese, and baked in the oven until the cheese is perfectly melted. What makes this dish great is that the sauce bakes into the noodles, giving it a completely different flavor.

Tasting Guidelines

Taste is **savory**, meaty, and cheesey.

Weight is **heavy** but can be balanced with spicy, vinegar, and sugar.

Texture is **soft** and noodley.

For **low to moderate** side effects.

Emotional response of a **good Italian meal.**

Best categorized as family style **Italian food.**

Ingredients

1 lb. ground turkey, 90/10 lean ground beef, or Italian sausage, browned with grease drained

1 c. Parmesan cheese, shredded *(don't be cheap get the good stuff, something aged at least eighteen months like Parmesano Reggiano)*

1 lb. fresh mozzarella, sliced into thin circles

1 box penne or mostaccioli, cooked *(I prefer Barilla)*

1 yellow onion, chopped and sauteed

1 batch marinara sauce *(follow recipe in this book)*

Flavor Balancers

1 tsp. kosher salt

1/2 tbsp. black pepper

Aromatics

1 tbsp. garlic, minced

1/2 tbsp. dried oregano

4 fresh basil leaves, chopped

Recipe Directions

Preheat oven to 375°F. Move fresh mozzarella and fresh basil to the side. Combine all remaining ingredients in a large mixing bowl, making certain to mix all ingredients thoroughly. Pack mixture into suitably sized casserole dish. Cover with fresh mozzarella slices, and bake until mozzarella is thoroughly melted and center of casserole has reached 145°F. Remove from oven, garnish with fresh basil, and serve with Parmesan cheese and crusty bread.

Chef Tips

If you live in the Saint Louis area and have the opportunity, substitute the fresh mozzarella for provel. You'll thank me later. You can also use any kind of tasty, melty cheeses like Gruyère, taleggio, or ricotta salata. I highly recommend getting a hold of some high quality pecorino romano and hand grating it in place of the Parmesan.

Pasta Alla Marco

Recipe Description

Pasta Alla Marco is a fun and sassy pasta dish that adds variety to everyday pasta. Its bright color and fun textures make eating pasta fun and delicious.

Tasting Guidelines

Taste is **savory,** sweet, and a little spicy.

Weight is **light to medium** but can be balanced with vinegar and sugar.

Texture is **soft** and noodley.

For **low to moderate** treatment side effects.

Emotional response of **summer time fun.**

Best categorized as **modern Italian cuisine.**

Ingredients

2 links, or 4 oz., spicy salsicca

1 box Barrilla bow tie pasta

1 can diced tomatoes

1/2 red onion, cut into thin strips

1 red pepper, cut in thin strips

1 tbsp. olive oil

Parmesan, optional

Flavor Balancers

1 tsp. kosher salt

1 cup red wine *(Chianti is preferred)*

1/2 tbsp. black pepper

2 tbsp. red wine vinegar

2 tbsp. sugar

Aromatics

2 tbsp. garlic, minced

1 tsp. dried oregano

Recipe Directions

In a 2 qt. sauce pan, heat oil to a medium heat. Add sausage, garlic, onion, and red peppers. Sauté until onions are translucent. Add red wine and mix thoroughly, allowing red pepper and onions to soak up the wine. Add salt, black pepper, red wine vinegar, sugar, oregano, and tomatoes. Stir well and cover.

Allow to work on stove top for 45 minutes over medium heat, stirring every few minutes to avoid burning the tomatoes. Ten minutes before sauce is finished, prepare noodles in well salted water. *(Water should taste like the ocean.)* Prepare pasta as directed on box. Do not allow to over cook. Drain pasta and lightly cover with olive oil, mixing to avoid sticking. Return pasta to pot, making sure not to place the pot back on the hot burner. At this point, you want to taste the sauce; add extra sugar if it's too acidic. After sauce is satisfactory, toss pasta with sauce and serve.

Chef Tips

Don't be alarmed if the sauce turns out thin with chunks of tomato. This is what we are looking for. Also, cheap, low-quality pastas will be mushy so get a good quality pasta because you need a firm texture.

Pot Roast

Recipe Description

Pot roast is an American classic found everywhere from restaurants to the frozen food isle. It is comprised of a slow cooked chunk of meat, suspended in liquid, and surrounded by vegetables and potatoes.

Tasting Guidelines

Taste is warm, **savory,** hearty, and filling.

Weight is **heavy** but can be balanced with vinegar.

Texture is **soft.**

For people with **low to moderate** chemotherapy side effects.

Emotional response of **home-cooked love.**

Best categorized as a **comfort food.**

Ingredients

2 lbs. chuck roast, rump roast, or round roast if less-fatty meat is desire

3 carrots, chopped

1 yellow onion, quartered into wedges *(think like Chinese food)*

6 small red potatoes, quartered

3 celery stalks, chopped

1 c. water

2 small cans beef consume

1 tbsp. cornstarch

Flavor Balancers

kosher salt to taste

black pepper to taste

2 tbsp. red wine vinegar

2 tbsp. sugar

Aromatics

2 tbps. garlic, minced

2 bay leaves

1 sprig fresh rosemary, with the needles crushed to release the oils

Recipe Directions

Step one for the rosemary: remove rosemary needles from stem. Using a large chef's knife on a cutting board of suitable size, utilize the flat part of the blade to crush and drag the rosemary needles. Doing this will release more of its fantastic oil, creating an extremely aromatic dish.

Next, cover all surfaces of the roast with salt and pepper. Bring a large skillet to high heat. Take roast and brown all sides of roast, allowing to cook until each side gets a nice char on it. *(Think nice steak)* When all sides are sufficiently brown, transfer into a large slow cooker. Add remaining ingredients. Cook on high about four hours or for a slower cook method, cook on low 8-10 hours until meat is tender and falls apart. After roast is tender, slice for serving when appropriate. *(Think Thanksgiving turkey)*

Chef Tips

Use beef round instead of chuck if it is difficult for heavier foods to be kept down. A chuck roast is fattier and therefore will yield a more tender finished product. So this is usually recommended. My favorite part about this recipe is that it is actually two dishes in one. Whatever you have that is leftover can be left in the pot and additional veggies can be added and more soup base or water and left to cook on night over low to have a wonderful beef stew in the morning! If stew is too heavy, add red wine vinegar or red wine vinaigrette. Don't be afraid to add a healthy dose of sugar to make the stew more appealing to your loved one. A couple of dashes of red pepper flakes really fill out this recipe, hitting all those flavor senses.

Ratatouille

Recipe Description

A classic southern French dish often categorized as a peasant food because of its low cost and lack of meat in the dish. Made famous by the movie of the same name, this dish is indeed fantastic.

Tasting Guidelines

Taste is **savory.**
Weight is **light** but can be balanced with savory.
Texture is **soft.**
For **low to moderate** treatment side effects.
Emotional response of **home cooked love.**
Best categorized as **classic French.**

Ingredients

1 medium eggplant *(aubergine)*
1 lb. zucchini *(courgette)*, quartered
2 green bell peppers, cut into strips
1 red bell pepper, cut into strips
1 large can tomatoes, diced
2 large red onions, sliced
1/2 cup olive oil

Flavor Balancers

kosher salt *(lots of it)*
2 tbsp. dark soy sauce
black pepper to taste
2 tbsp. red wine vinegar
2 tbsp. sugar

Aromatics

2 tbsp. garlic, minced
1 whole bay leaf
1 tbsp. dried oregano
2 tbsp. Italian flat leaf parsley, chopped
1 tbsp. fresh basil leaves, chopped

Recipe Directions

The very first step in this recipe is to do what I call "defunking" the eggplant. Eggplant is a naturally bitter food. So to avoid this, we have to do a small amount of additional prep to remove the funkiness and end up with a delicious savory product. Slice the eggplant into quarter inch thick circles. Then take a colander and line it with paper towels. Sprinkle a little bit of salt on the paper. Now pick up our first slice of eggplant and sprinkle salt on both sides. Lay it down in colander. Pick up your second slice of eggplant and repeat salting method and lay on top of previous placed eggplant slice. Repeat this method, making layers of eggplant and salting in between each layer as you stack. Allow colander to sit in a sanitized sink for at least 30 minutes while eggplant is defunking.

While eggplant is defunking, preheat oven to 375°F. After 30 minutes, rinse your eggplant thoroughly, and cut the rounds into quarters. Now mix all ingredients into large mixing bowl. Transfer to casserole dish. You may need several. Bake at 375°F until juices from vegetables have baked off and ratatouille has a thick consistency, about 1 hour and 30 minutes. Serve with crusty bread and cheese.

Chef Tips

If you do this in a slow cooker, do not use diced tomatoes as there is too much liquid. Use about 6 Roma *(plum)* tomatoes cut into 1/8 wedges.

Ratatouille, Greek

Ease of Preparation
Level 2-Intermediate

Recipe Description
Very similar in construction to the French version but with a Greek twist. It features the addition of bell peppers, Feta cheese, potatoes, and, if you are feeling up to it, chicken. This makes it a much heartier meal.

Tasting Guidelines
Taste is savory and hearty.
Weight is light but can be balanced with savory.
Texture is soft.
For people with low to moderate treatment side effects.
Emotional response of home cooked goodness.
Best categorized as classic home style Greek.

Ingredients
8 oz. feta cheese, crumbled
1 medium oval eggplant *(aubergine)*
1 lb. zucchini *(courgette)*, cut into quarters
1 lb. red potatoes, cubed
1 green bell pepper, sliced into this strips
1 red bell pepper, sliced into thin strips
1 large can tomatoes diced
8 oz. Portabella mushrooms, sliced
2 large red onion, sliced
1/2 cup olive oil

Optional
2 chicken breast, raw and cubed

Garnish
Crusty bread to serve *(This is optional. It depends on the severity of mouth sores when you make this dish.)*

Flavor Balancers

kosher salt
2 tbsp. soy sauce
1/2 tbsp. freshly ground black pepper
8 shakes red pepper flakes
2 tbsp. red wine vinegar
2 tbsp. sugar

Aromatics

2 tbsp. minced garlic
1 tbsp. dried oregano
2 tbsp. Italian flat leaf parsley, chopped

Recipe Directions

The very first step in this recipe is to do what I call "defunking" the eggplant. Eggplant is a naturally bitter food. So to avoid this, we have to do a small amount of additional prep to remove the funkiness and end up with a delicious savory product. Slice the eggplant into quarter inch thick circles. Then take a colander and line it with paper towels. Sprinkle a little bit of salt on the paper. Now pick up our first slice of eggplant and sprinkle salt on both sides. Lay it down in colander. Pick up your second slice of eggplant and repeat salting method and lay on top of previous placed eggplant slice. Repeat this method, making layers of eggplant and salting in between each layer as you stack. Allow colander to sit in a sanitized sink for at least 30 minutes while eggplant is defunking.

While eggplant is defunking, preheat oven to 375°F. After 30 minutes, rinse your eggplant thoroughly, and cut the rounds into quarters. Now mix all ingredients into large mixing bowl. Transfer to casserole dish. You may need several. Bake at 375°F until juices from vegetables have baked off and ratatouille has a thick consistency, about 1 hour and 30 minutes. Serve with crusty bread and cheese.

Chef Tips

If you do this in a slow cooker, do not use diced tomatoes, as there is too much liquid. Use about 6 Roma tomatoes cut into 1/8 wedges.

Spaghetti and Meatballs

Ease of Preparation
Level 2-Intermediate

Recipe Description
What would a cookbook be without a decent recipe for spaghetti and meatballs? My father-in-law, Tony's favorite recipe. When he first had this dish, he was immediately transported back to his childhood. Growing up in an Italian family, he immediately declared that Me Maw would be very proud! This is also one of my mom's favorite dishes and something she asked for weekly when she was going through chemo treatments. Jarred Sauce? FAH' GET' ABOUT IT! *(Throw up hands in the air!)* Don't be chintzy! Make my marinara recipe in this book! Take the time and do it right!

Tasting Guidelines
Taste is **savory and sweet.**
Weight is **medium** but can be balanced with lemon juice.
Texture is **soft.**
For **low to moderate** treatment side effects.
Emotional response of a **good family meal.**
Best categorized as **Italian.**

Ingredients
2 lbs. spaghetti noodles, medium bodied, not thin and not thick
1 batch marinara *(follow recipe in this book)*
cooking spray
olive oil
kosher salt

Meatball Ingredients
1 lb. pork, ground
1 lb. 90/10 lean ground beef
½ cup grated Parmesan cheese
2 eggs
bread crumbs as needed

Flavor Balancers

1/2 tbsp. kosher salt
1/2 tbsp. black pepper
2–4 shakes crushed red pepper
2 tbsp. lemon juice
2 tbsp. red wine vinaigrette dressing

Aromatics

2 tbsp. garlic, minced
1 tbsp. dried oregano

Recipe Directions

Mix all of the above meatball ingredients, flavor balancers, and aromatics, in a large bowl. Mix by hand, thoroughly distributing all ingredients. Mix in bread crumbs as necessary to absorb extra moisture. Cover and allow to rest in refrigerator for at least 2 hours.

Preheat oven to 425°F. After meatball mixture is done marinating, roll by hand into your desired size. I prefer to make mine about the size of a golf ball. Now place into a 9x13 baking dish. Make sure that your dish is well coated with cooking spray. After filling dish with meatballs, spray the top of the meatballs with nice even coat of the same cooking spray. Bake until juices run clear and a little bit of the cheese starts melting out. This will vary based on the size of your meatballs. If they are the golf ball size, about 30–45 minutes. If your meatballs are larger, they will take longer.

During last 15 minutes, cook off your spaghetti. Making sure that the water you use is salted enough to taste like the ocean. Don't over cook your pasta. Strain well and lightly coat with olive oil to avoid sticking.

Chef Tips

Some people cook their meatballs in their sauce. I don't do this as you cannot get a good browning on the meatballs, which reduces the savory flavor of the dish. Another reason to bake the meatballs off in the oven, besides the additional savory characteristics, is you can cook off much of the grease. This contributes to a lighter weight meatball. Remember that lighter dishes are easier for chemo patients to eat.

Spaghetti Ala Bolognese

Ease of Preparation
Level 2-Intermediate

Recipe Description
Very simply translated: spaghetti in the style of the Bolognese. The Bolognese are famous for their meat sauce. And it is fabulous over spaghetti.

Tasting Guidelines
Taste is **savory and sweet.**
Weight is **medium** but can be balanced with vinegar or lemon juice.
Texture is **soft** and noodley.
For **low to moderate** treatment side effects.
Emotional response of a **hearty Italian meal.**
Best categorized as **classic Italian.**

Ingredients
2 lbs. thick spaghetti noodles
1 batch marinara *(follow recipe in this book)*
1 lb. Italian sausage, ground

Flavor Balancers
kosher salt

Recipe Directions
Brown the sausage in a pan. Drain the grease. Stir in the marinara sauce. Allow to simmer for 30 minutes on a low heat. Allow all flavors to work together.

Boil noodles in water that tastes as salty as the ocean. Serve with Parmesan. Enjoy.

SIDES

Cauliflower Sauté

Recipe Description
Tender cauliflower tossed in a sweet and savory sauce. This is a modified Chinese recipe made for use in the average American kitchen.

Tasting Guidelines
Taste is **sweet and savory.**
Weight is **light** but can be balanced with vinegar.
Texture is **soft** with a little crunch.
For **low to moderate** treatment side effects.
Emotional response of a **refreshing change of pace.**
Best categorized as **American.**

Ingredients
1 head of cauliflower
1 tbsp. olive oil

Flavor Balancers
1 tbsp. soy sauce
1/2 tbsp. red wine vinegar
1 tbsp. sugar

Aromatics
1/2 tbsp. garlic, minced

Recipe Directions
Steam the cauliflower until tender. In large sauce pan, heat oil to a medium heat. Sauté garlic to a light golden brown. Next, add cauliflower. Sauté cauliflower with garlic. Add remainder of ingredients and seasonings. Cook water out of sauce. Toss cauliflower in sauce until the sauce adheres to the cauliflower. Serve and enjoy.

Cheesy Potatoes

Recipe Description

An old family recipe. No meal in my family is complete with out these cheesy potatoes. I'll never forget the year when my uncle declared he did not like the cheesy potatoes and had never liked the cheesy potatoes after 30 years of eating them. We were all in shock. The only thought that came to mind was, How could you not like these? So now I leave this up to you to decide. Are you pro or anti cheesy potatoes?

Tasting Guidelines

Taste is **savory** and cheesy.
Weight is **heavy** but can be balanced with vinegar.
Texture is **soft** with a little crunch on top.
For **low** treatment side effects.
Emotional response of a **delicious home cooked meal.**
Best categorized as **classic southern fare.**

Ingredients

8 oz. sharp cheddar cheese, shredded
1 bag frozen potatoes O'Brien
1/2 yellow onion, diced
8 ounces sour cream
1 can cream of mushroom soup

Flavor Balancers

1/2 tbsp. salt
1 tbsp. black pepper
5 shakes red pepper flakes
1/2 tbsp. red wine vinegar
2 tsp. sugar

Aromatics

1/2 tbsp. garlic, minced

Recipe Directions

Preheat your oven to 425°F. In a large mixing bowl, combine all ingredients and seasonings and stir thoroughly. Place contents into 9x13 baking dish. Bake uncovered until all surfaces and edges are golden brown, about 45 minutes to an hour. Remove from the oven and stir well before serving.

Grandma's Cast-Iron Skillet Cornbread

Recipe Description
An American country classic. Cooking cornbread in a cast iron skillet takes it to a whole new level. The addition of honey and sugar in the cornbread also helps compensate for the dryness that cornbread is typically plagued by.

Tasting Guidelines
Taste is **sweet.**
Weight is **medium** but can be balanced with sugar and butter.
Texture is **soft but mealy.**
For **low to moderate** treatment side effects.
Emotional response of **grandma's home cooking.**
Best categorized as **American southern-style cooking.**

Ingredients
2 boxes of corn bread mix *(make per box instructions)*
4 oz butter *(1 stick)*

Flavor Balancers
1/2 cup sugar
1/2 cup honey

Recipe Directions

Preheat your oven to 425°F and place the skillet into the oven for at least 20 minutes to allow it to completely come to temperature. Prepare cornbread mix as directed on the packaging, adding the additional sugar and honey into the mix. Remove iron skillet from oven and immediately pour batter into the heated skillet. Bake at 425°F until cooked thoroughly. When finished, top with real butter and a light sprinkling of sugar. Add 2 tbsp. extra liquid to compensate for sugar and honey.

Chef Tips

Add 2 tbsp. extra liquid to compensate for the extra sugar and honey.

Corn Casserole

Dish Description

Another classic American southern style dish. The brilliance of this dish is its simplicity. It is almost as if somebody looked in the cupboard and asked, "I wonder what would happen if I mixed these ingredients together?" Nonetheless, a delightfully delicious and addictive side dish.

Tasting Guidelines

Taste is **sweet and savory.**

Weight is **heavy** but can be balanced with vinegar.

Texture is **soft.**

For **low to moderate** treatment side effects.

Emotional response of **delicious homecooking.**

Best categorized as **American, southern style.**

Ingredients

1 c. cheddar cheese, shredded

1 package corn muffin mix, mixed according to directions

1 can creamed corn

8 oz. sour cream

Flavor Balancers

1/4 cup sugar

Recipe Directions

Combine all ingredients together in bread pan and bake at 375°F until golden brown on top and an inserted tooth pick comes out clean, about 30 minutes.

Perfect Mashed Potatoes

Recipe Description

These mashed potatoes are exactly as advertised. They are perfect. Not too heavy. Not too light. Perfectly savory.

Tasting Guidelines

Taste is **savory.**

Weight is **medium** but can be balanced with salt.

Texture is **soft.**

For **low to severe** treatment side effects.

Emotional response of a good **home cooked meal.**

Best categorized as **classic American.**

Ingredients

2 1/2 lbs. Yukon gold potatoes *(yellow waxy skinned potatoes)*

1/2 c. heavy whipping cream

2 tbsp. Parmesan cheese

2 oz. unsalted butter *(½ stick)*

1/2 c. sour cream

Flavor Balancers

kosher salt to taste

black pepper to taste

Recipe Directions

Chunk up potatoes into small pieces, leaving the skin on. Boil on high for 35–45 minutes or until tender. Strain water from potatoes, and place potatoes back in pot. Add remaining ingredients. Mash by hand or by a hand mixer to desired consistency.

Chef Tips

If potatoes are too thin, heat potatoes on medium heat until thickened. Stir regularly to prevent burning. If potatoes are too thick, add more cream or milk. Salt and pepper to taste.

Roasted Red Potatoes with Cheese

Recipe Description
Good old-fashioned roasted potatoes with a twist.

Tasting Guidelines
Taste is **savory.**
Weight is **medium** but can be balanced with salt.
Texture is **crunchy.**
For **low to moderate** treatment side effects.
Emotional response of **mmmmm... this is good.**
Best categorized as **American.**

Ingredients
2 1/2 lbs. red potatoes, medium diced
1/4 c. Parmesan cheese
1/4 c. cheddar cheese
1/4 cup feta
2 tbsp. olive oil

Flavor Balancers
kosher salt to taste
black pepper to taste
1 tsp. cayenne pepper

Aromatics
1/2 tbsp. dried garlic

Recipe Directions
Toss all ingredients, except the cheeses, in a big mixing bowl. Bake in preheated oven at 425°F for about 45 minutes to an hour on a large baking sheet. During the last 10 minutes of cooking, pull potatoes out of oven and sprinkle with Parmesan, cheddar, and feta. Place back in oven to finish. Serve and eat.

Homemade Spanish Rice

Recipe Description

Classic Spanish rice not from a box? Yes. You can definitely make Spanish rice at home all on your own with this super easy recipe.

Tasting Guidelines

Taste is lightly **savory and aromatic.**
Weight is **light** but can be balanced with salt.
Texture is **soft.**
For **low to moderate** treatment side effects.
Emotional response of a **night out at a Mexican restaurant.**
Best categorized as **classic Spanish.**

Ingredients

1 c. generic white rice
1 small can tomatoes, diced
1 tbsp. olive oil
1 1/2 c. chicken stock

Flavor Balancers

2 tsp. kosher salt
2 tsp. black pepper
2 tsp. chili powder

Aromatics

1/2 tbsp. garlic, minced
1 tsp. oregano, dried

Recipe Directions

Combine all ingredients in rice cooker and turn on. Mix well before serving.

Chef Tips

If you don't have a rice cooker, go buy one. Right now.

SAUCES

Marinara, Home-style

Ease of Preparation
Level 2-Intermediate

Recipe Description
A classic marinara sauce made with approval from my wife's Sicilian family. Savory and aromatic with sweetness to balance out the acidity of the natural tomatoes.

Tasting Guidelines
Taste is **savory, sweet, and aromatic.**
Weight of this dish is **light** but can be balanced with sugar.
Texture of this dish is **saucy.**
For people with **low to severe treatment** side effects.
Emotional response of **home cooked goodness.**
Best categorized as **classic Italian fare.**

Ingredients
2 large cans tomatoes, diced
1 tbsp. olive oil

Flavor Balancers
kosher salt to taste
2 c. Chianti *(red wine)*
black pepper to taste
1 tsp. cayenne pepper or 2 firm shakes
of red pepper flakes
2 tbsp. red wine vinegar
1/4 cup sugar

Aromatics
2 tbsp. garlic, minced
1/2 tbsp. oregano
fresh basil *(optional and added at the end)*

Recipe Directions

Take a 2 qt. sauce pan and bring to medium heat. Sauté the garlic in the olive oil until lightly brown. Immediately add oregano, red pepper, and red wine to stop the garlic from processing any further. Allow wine to reduce for 10 minutes. Add salt, black pepper, red wine vinegar, and tomatoes. Stir well. Allow to simmer over medium heat uncovered for 45 minutes to an hour, stirring frequently to avoid burning. After 45 minutes, take a whisk and using a whisking/mashing motion break down the tomatoes until it begins to look more like marinara sauce.

As you break down the tomato chunks, they will mix with the tomato juice and will naturally thicken the sauce. Add sugar and allow to simmer 15 more minutes, and then begin the final seasoning process. Add more salt, sugar, and black pepper as necessary. If sauce is acidic and makes the back of your tongue or mouth feel dry, add sugar in small increments, stirring the sauce thoroughly to melt the sugar into the sauce. For a rustic or home-style marinara, whisking should be sufficient to attain the desired consistency. If a more commercial-looking sauce is desired, blend the diced tomatoes in a blender before adding them to the pot.

Chef Tips

You never want your marinara to be bright red. Any marinara sauce that is bright red has not been cooked for long enough for the truly savory aspects of the tomatoes to be released. Therefore, you look for a deeper red similar to a burgundy to tell that the sauce is truly finished. Never ever ever ever cook your marinara sauce over high heat because plain and simply you will burn it! Slow and low is the tempo. It is better to slowly prepare your marinara than to burn it.

You also need to make certain that you have a nice, thick-bottomed pot. A thin pot will absolutely burn the sauce before the top of your sauce even gets warm. If you are terrified of burning the sauce, you can always make it in a slow cooker on low heat and let it work over night.

Marsala Wine Sauce

Dish Description

A classic Italian sauce made from butter, mushrooms, chicken stock, and a unique wine. Done correctly, this sauce is savory, sweet, and very rich. It pairs well with most anything. When paired with the Pork or Chicken Scaloppine, it becomes the key ingredient in making chicken or pork Marsala. It is especially good on potatoes.

Tasting Guidelines

Taste is **savory, sweet, and rich.**
Weight is **medium** but can be balanced vinegar or lemon juice.
Texture is **soft** and saucy.
For **low to moderate** treatment side effects.
Emotional response of **delicious Italian food.**
Best categorized as **classic Italian fare.**

Ingredients

8 oz. portabella mushrooms, finely chopped
32 oz. chicken stock
1 stick butter
flour

Flavor Balancers

1 tsp. kosher salt
1–2 c. Marsala wine
2 tsp. black pepper
2 tsp. red pepper
2 tbsp. red wine vinegar
sugar as needed

Aromatics

2 tbsp. garlic, minced
2 tsp. oregano
2 tsp. rosemary
1 tsp. thyme

Recipe Directions

In a large sauté pan, melt the butter at medium heat. Add mushrooms and garlic; sauté until mushrooms are thoroughly cooked and have almost dissolved into mush. Add oregano, rosemary, thyme, black pepper, and red pepper. Increase heat to a high heat, quickly stir in flour until butter is absorbed. Immediately add wine and deglaze the pan, stirring thoroughly and quickly. Allow the wine to reduce to a thin sauce. Add vinegar and chicken stock, stirring well.

Reduce heat to medium-heat, and allow to work uncovered at least 45 minutes, tasting often. If your sauce is not naturally sweet, you have gotten a bad batch of wine and will need to add sugar to compensate. The sauce should be lightly sweet, very savory, and aromatic. Serve over scaloppine, with your preference of sides. I like mashed potatoes, broccoli, and crusty bread.

Orange Sauce

Dish Description
A sweet and savory sauce. Perfect over grilled, roasted, and fried meats.

Tasting Guidelines
Taste is **sweet and savory.**
Weight is **light** but can be balanced with sugar.
Texture is **soft** and saucy.
For **low to moderate** treatment side effects.
Emotional response of a **fun, sweet citrusy sauce.**
Best categorized as **Mediterranean/Chinese fusion.**

Ingredients
2 oranges

Flavor Balancers
kosher salt to taste
2 tbsp. light soy sauce
1 tbsp. dark soy sauce
black pepper to taste
2 tsp. red pepper flakes
1 tbsp. red wine vinegar
1 c. orange juice
1 c. sugar

Aromatics
1 tsp. ground ginger

Recipe Directions

In a medium sauce pan, combine orange juice, red pepper flakes, dark and light soy sauce, red wine vinegar, and ginger. Bring to a medium heat; allow to simmer 10 minutes. Take one orange and cut in half. Squeeze fresh juice into sauce, taking care to strain the seeds. Place orange rind into sauce. Allow to simmer 10 additional minutes.

Remove rind. Slowly whisk in sugar. Taste for sweetness. Slice and serve with fresh orange slices as garnish.

Chef Tips

This sauce is wonderful over roasted pork loin or chicken breasts. It is also suitable for use in the classic Chinese dishes orange chicken, orange beef, orange pork.

Pesto

Dish Description

A northern Italian favorite. A simple sauce made from basil leaves. It is incredibly versatile and can be placed on anything that is of a lighter weight. Especially good with chicken. Pesto was huge in the '80s and '90s, which was captured in the iconic sitcom Seinfeld where George *(paraphrased)* says, "Ya know? I just don't care for pesto."

Tasting Guidelines

Taste is **clean.**
Weight is **light** but can be balanced with Parmesan.
Texture is **soft and saucy.**
For people with **low to severe** treatment side effects.
Emotional response of feeling **clean and refreshed.**
Best categorized as **northern Italian.**

Ingredients

1 lb. fresh basil leaves
1/2 c. extra virgin olive oil
1/2 c. Parmesan
2 tbsp. pine nuts *(optional)*
2 tbsp. garlic, minced *(optional)*

Recipe Directions

Place basil, garlic, Parmesan and pine nuts into blender. Pulse the blender until basil is finely chopped. Add olive oil until it forms a saucy consistency. May require more olive oil than the recipe calls for.

Chef Tips

Pesto is actually a real nice, light sauce. It has tons of uses. You can put it on pasta, sandwiches, toast, brush it on chicken, and even substitute it in any recipe that fresh basil is required. For example, in Caprese salad, you can substitute pesto instead of fresh basil leaves and toss with balsamic vinegar instead of red wine vinaigrette for a change of pace.

Plum Sauce

Dish Description

A classic Spanish sauce. Mostly unheard of in the United States. The sauce is sweet, tangy, and savory. The best way to describe this sauce is that it is like a Spanish barbecue sauce. The dried plums take care of the consistency and thickness of the sauce, eliminating the need for a thickener. The dried plums are also great for digestion. This is an added benefit as chemotherapy can cause problems in this area. Use this sauce over grilled foods for best results.

Tasting Guidelines

Taste is **savory and sweet.**
Weight is **medium** but can be balanced with savory and sweet.
Texture is **soft and saucy.**
For people with **low to moderate** treatment side effects.
Emotional response of eating a **tasty barbecue sauce.**
Best categorized as **classic Spanish.**

Ingredients

8 oz. pitted prunes *(dried plums)*
1 c. water

Flavor Balancers

1 tsp. kosher salt
1/2 cup red wine or sherry
2 tsp. freshly ground black pepper
1 tbsp. red wine vinegar
1 tbsp. sugar

Aromatics

1 sprig of rosemary
1 tsp. cinnamon

Recipe Directions

In a medium sauce pan, combine the prunes, cinnamon, salt, black pepper, red wine, rosemary, and water. Bring to a boil until prunes have re-hydrated. Then, using a whisk, mash the prunes until they have become more liquefied and mix well. Add one tbsp. of red wine vinegar and sugar. Whisk well and allow to simmer for 5–10 minutes. Taste sauce and adjust seasonings as necessary. Sauce should taste like savory sugared plums with a bit of dryness on the back.

Chef Tips

This sauce is amazing! Prunes are also packed with potassium, B12, B6, fiber, and an enzyme that helps re-hydrate your intestines, making it easier to go to the bathroom. Don't be afraid of this sauce because of the prunes. The added sugar and cinnamon really livens it up. And you will be glad you ate this! This recipe is also great for people who are getting backed up and bloated. This sauce is a great all natural way to help get things moving along. *Wink.*

Tzatziki Sauce

Dish Description
A classic Greek yogurt sauce typically associated with gyro sandwiches *(doner kebabs.)* This recipe is fabulous, not just on sandwiches but also served on bread, pitas, or over a salad as a dressing. The versatility of this sauce is amazing. Given its yogurt-based construction, you would assume it is heavy when in fact it is very light. The vinegar in this dish helps settle your stomach, and the active yogurt cultures will help get your belly back under control.

Tasting Guidelines
Taste is **savory, sweet, and tangy.**
Weight is **light** but can be balanced with honey.
Texture is **soft and creamy.**
For people with **low to severe** treatment side effects.
Emotional response of **unexpected yumminess.**
Best categorized as **Greek.**

Ingredients
1 large tub honeyed Greek yogurt
1 large cucumber, peeled and diced
3 Roma tomatoes, diced
1/2 medium sized red onion, diced

Flavor Balancers
kosher salt to taste
black pepper to taste
1/4 cup red wine vinaigrette dressing *(I always use Wishbone brand. It's my favorite.)*

Aromatics
1 tbsp. garlic, minced

Garnish
crusty break or pita bread to serve

Recipe Directions

Take cucumber, tomatoes, and red onion and place in a large mixing bowl. Shake red wine vinaigrette dressing well and coat thoroughly. Sprinkle in salt, pepper, and garlic. Allow to marinate at room temperature at least one hour, stirring frequently or in the refrigerator for two hours. Mix in yogurt. Toss gently. Allow to marinate in refrigerator until flavors become cohesive.

Chef Tips

The longer the flavors have to sit together the more cohesive they become. If flavors do not emphasize the sweetness, stir in honey until you reach desired sweetness. Serve with fresh pitas or fresh bread. It also makes a fantastic dressing for salads and can be eaten as a condiment over falafel, gyros, other sandwiches, just eaten by itself, or over oatmeal. If mouth sores are problematic, you can puree the cucumber, onions, and tomatoes for a much softer texture.

192

SOUPS

According to Auguste Escoffier, the father of modern western culinary theory, there are nine main categories of soups. For ease and simplicity, I have organized soups into four categories. I simply wanted to provide this to help spark ideas in your head of different types of soups and stews you can make.

Thin Soups

Broths, consume, vegetable, and lentil are all thin soups. Start here when you have somebody who cannot eat! Since these are lighter in weight and flavor, they can be eaten even by the most finicky eater. They are also fantastic for someone with an upset stomach. Great for someone who is cold and needs to warm up. And, it is just a great place to start to get calories into somebody. If somebody wants tea, coffee, or soda, it is better to give them a cup of warm broth to drink. Those other beverages have no caloric or nutritional value.

Thick Soups *(cream soups, pureed, bisque, and chowders)*

Thick soups are any soups that are heavier in nutrients and weight. They are still lighter than eating a full meal, but are heavier in nutrients than a thin soup. Some great examples of thick soups are crab bisque, clam chowder, chili, cream of broccoli, split pea soup, potato soup, and beer-cheese soup.

Cold Soups *(soups you can serve cold)*

Cold soups are great for people who have mouth sores. The great part about cold soups is they can be thick or thin, and heavy or light. You can get crazy and creative with them. Some examples of cold soups are gazpacho, cold potato leek soup, and fresh peach and yogurt soup.

Stews

Stews are the classic cold air dish. They are savory and flavorful by nature. They also tend to be pretty heavy. The beautiful thing about a stew is its ease and convenience.

Anybody can make a stew! You can also turn other meals leftovers, like pot roast, into a stew very easily. And the best part is, you can make them in the slow cooker! Oh, the luxury of set and forget!

Thickeners

Thickeners are heavily employed in the making of soups, stews, and sauces. The purpose of a thickener is exactly what it sounds like; to make items thicker in density. The following are commonly used thickeners and their benefits.

Cornstarch

Cornstarch is a fantastic thickener for just about any application. It is mixed with cold water before being swirled into a hot dish. After the cornstarch is added, the dish is typically returned to or very near a boil for the cornstarch's thickening properties to be activated. One of the side effects of using cornstarch is that is will tend to make whatever dish you use it in a little cloudy. And as such, it is fairly evident when cornstarch has been used.

Note: Soups and sauces thickened with cornstarch are not as cloudy as when you use a roux.

Tapioca Flour

Tapioca flour is a thickener, that when employed, tends to be very clear. As such, it is the traditional thickener of fruit pies and fruit tarts.

Potato Starch

Potato starch is a thickener that is very similar to cornstarch in both its application and its thickening properties. The main difference is potato starch remains clear when used, whereas cornstarch does not. Potato starch loses its thickening properties as it chills. Potatoes in your dish, when cooked in your meal, will naturally add potato starch. This will help thicken the dish when it's put in automatically.

Rice Flour

Rice flour is very similar to wheat flour in its thickening properties. It tends to be cloudy or opaque. Just like potato starch, adding rice to a dish will naturally thicken a dish when allowed to cook long enough.

Wheat Flour

Wheat flour *(or Roux)* is a thickener traditionally used in cream-based sauces. Think white country gravy. It should always be employed by cooking it into fatty oils. If you don't cook it into fatty oils and simply add raw flour to your dishes, the dish will end up being chunky and will taste like uncooked flour. Wheat flour is a cloudy or opaque thickener. It is used in conditions where having a clear sauce or liquid is not important. Wheat flour is typically mixed with melted butter to prepare a mixture it is known as roux. The great thing about roux is that you can make a large batch of it. Roll it onto a piece of wax paper like cookie dough. Then, slice it into squares like brownies to be used later. It can also be frozen or refrigerated for long periods of time, making it very convenient to use.

How To Make A Roux

Pronounced Roo

In a medium sauce pan, melt butter over medium heat. When butter is thoroughly melted, stir in flour until all butter has been absorbed by flour. Stir thoroughly and be careful not to burn. Allow mixture to remain over heat for 30 seconds to cook the flour flavor out. Immediately remove mixture from heat and set to side for later use.

A textbook definition of roux would call for half flour, half butter. But in real life application, roux turns out better when it is closer to 60 percent butter and 40 percent flour. Remember to slowly add the flour into the butter. What you want is for the flour to drink up the butter. When this has been achieved, stop adding flour.

When adding roux to a meal, follow these guidelines: Over medium-high heat, slowly add roux. Stir the roux into the soup until uniformly mixed. Allow soup to thicken until a desired consistency is reached. This process should happen in 2–3 minute increments. The method is add roux. Stir. Return to simmer while stirring. If the soup has not thickened sufficiently after returning to a simmer, add roux and repeat the process. Do not allow soup to boil, and do not allow it to burn. If a cream-based soup boils, it will break and separate entirely. This will cause it to instantly thin. If you burn it, the entire batch is ruined. So please, take your time with this process.

Soup Preparation

Soups can be made either on the stove or in a slow cooker. Some soups come out fantastic when a combination method is used where you prepare the base of the soup on the stove, then let the flavors combine, and finish in a slow cooker. I am a huge fan of the slow cooker method of cooking. I have found it to be a great tool when you need to make a large amount of something delicious but don't have time to always be stirring and watching the stove! All of these soup recipes can be made in a slow cooker. The difference would be simply combining all of the ingredients and letting the slow cooker work its magic. I personally like to use a combined method where I prepare the soup base on the stove. That way I can make certain that all of the flavors and textures are correct before letting the flavors set in.

Why do you have soups simmer for so long?

I like to have soups simmer for an extended amount of time because it allows the flavors to work together and become harmonious. The longer a dish cooks, the more blended the flavors become. A perfect example of this is chili. When you first make chili, it is very tasty. But when you refrigerate it and reheat it several times, you will notice that it gets better and better tasting. The reason for this is simply that the spices, flavors, and aromas have had sufficient time to commingle and become very friendly with each other! If you do not allow for a long simmer period, the flavors will not blend. The flavors will instead stand out as there own individual flavors and solitary items.

For example, in a Caprese salad *(tomato, mozzarella, and basil salad)*, the flavors in this dish are very strong on their own accord. When you layer them together, you get the savory flavor of the tomato, the creamy richness of the mozzarella, and the fresh licorice pop of the basil leaf completing the flavor. Each one of these flavors stand out on its own and is complimentary to the others. But ultimately, it is very unique and not blended.

In the blending of flavors, this is where the slow cooker really stands out. A slow cooker is a perfect, handy, easy-to-use tool for blending flavors. This is because of the simple fact that it is incredibly hard to burn something in a slow cooker. A burner can be too hot in one spot. Or, you can have a pot that is too thin and allows the soup to burn simply by too much heat transference. The slow cooker avoids this by two methods:

1) Being made of ceramic, heat is transferred evenly along the entire cooking surface. This allows for an even cook. Ceramic or earthenware cooking containers have been in use for thousands of years in all cultures all across the globe.

2) A slow cooker is surrounded by a heat jacket that allows for the heat to be transferred evenly along the entire container. A stock-pot on a stove only has one direction for heat to enter the dish, which is from the bottom.

The result is a fantastic cooking machine with a set-and-forget mentality. If you are hands-on like me, though, you may want to prepare the dish properly on the stove and then allow it to sit in a slow cooker to keep it warm all day. This is a fine technique too. No matter which way you go to let your flavors work together, *(as long as you mind your temperature, spices, and time)* you should end up with a very nice product that you and your loved ones are sure to enjoy.

Baked Potato Soup

Recipe Description

Baked potato soup is a lovely dish when you are in the mood for a hearty cup of soup. Very similar in construction to clam chowder. The appeal of baked potato soup is that without the seafood aspect, the dish looses its' pungency and becomes more approachable.

Tasting Guidelines

Taste is **savory.**

Weight is **medium** but can be balanced with red wine vinegar.

Texture is **soupy.**

For **low to moderate** treatment side effects.

Emotional response of having a **warm full belly.**

Best categorized as **classic American.**

Ingredients

2 c. sharp cheddar cheese, shredded
4 c. potatoes specifically yellow or red potatoes, diced
2 cans whole kernel corn, drained
1 c. carrots, diced
1 c. celery, diced
1 yellow onion, diced
1/4 cup green onions, sliced
2 large cans chicken broth
8 oz. butter *(2 sticks)*
4 c. whole milk
1/2 c. all purpose flour

Flavor Balancers

1 tsp. kosher salt
2 tbsp. black pepper
1 tbsp. red wine vinegar
1 tbsp. sugar

Aromatics

2 tbsp. garlic, minced
2 bay leaves
2 tbsp. Old Bay seasoning, optional but highly recommended

Garnish

1 c. crispy bacon, green onions, and sour cream, chopped for garnish

Recipe Directions

In a medium sauce pan, melt butter over medium heat. When butter is thoroughly melted, stir in flour until all butter has been absorbed by flour. Stir thoroughly and be careful not to burn. Allow mixture to remain over heat for 30 seconds to cook the flour flavor out. Immediately remove mixture from heat and set to side for later use.

Bring a large stock pot to medium heat and add oil. Then add garlic, celery, onions, and carrots. Cook over medium heat. Allow to cook until onions are translucent. Stir in potatoes, remaining seasonings, and chicken broth. Bring to a boil for 30 minutes or until potatoes become tender. In the microwave, cook the milk until warm but not boiling. Add to pot after potatoes are tender, making certain to stir in thoroughly. At this point, taste the soup and make any flavor adjustments necessary.

Over medium-high heat, slowly add roux and allow soup to thicken until a desired consistency is reached. This process should happen in 2–3 minute increments.

The method is: Add roux. Stir. Return to simmer while stirring. If after returning to a simmer, the soup has not thickened sufficiently, add roux and repeat process.

After soup is sufficiently thick, turn burner to low heat and slowly stir in cheddar cheese.
Serve with bread and garnishes.

Chef Tips

If soup is too heavy, add red wine vinegar. If soup does not feel full in flavor, it's missing sugar. If it doesn't taste savory, add a little MSG. If you are not concerned about color, instead of using MSG, add a little soy sauce instead. Soy sauce will darken the color of the soup.

Chicken and Dumplings

Ease of Preparation
Level 1-Easy

Recipe Description
Chicken and dumplings is the southern equivalent to chicken noodle soup. When you are sick or you do not feel good, nothing else will do. And nobody will ever make it better than your mom or grandma. But here is how I made it for my mom when she went through chemotherapy.

Tasting Guidelines
Taste is **savory** and aromatic.
Weight is **medium** but can be balanced with red wine vinegar.
Texture is **soft.**
For **low to moderate** treatment side effects.
Emotional response of a full belly and **home cooked love.**
Best categorized as **American-southern.**

Ingredients
2 lbs. chicken, shredded *(breasts or thighs depending on preference)*
1 pack frozen dumplings *(or you can make from scratch)*
1 bag frozen stew vegetables
1 c. cream *(optional)*
2 c. milk
1 large can chicken stock
1 c. water
4 oz. butter *(1 stick)*
1/2 cup flour

Flavor Balancers
1/2 tbsp. kosher salt
1/2 tbsp. black pepper
1 tsp. cayenne pepper
1 tbsp. red wine vinegar
2 tbsp. sugar

Aromatics
2 tsp. rosemary
1 tbsp. bay seasoning
1 tbsp. sage

Recipe Directions

In a large spaghetti pot, melt butter over medium heat. Add stew vegetables and cook until tender. Stir in flour to absorb extra butter. Mix in additional ingredients and seasonings, except dumplings. Allow to simmer 5 minutes to check seasoning levels. When proper seasoning levels have been reached, break and add frozen dumplings, slowly mixing to avoid sticking. Transfer to a slow cooker, and set on low heat and allow to work until dumplings begin to fall apart, about 2 hours. Change to the warm setting to avoid burning. Serve with cheddar cheese.

Chef Tips

There are two forms of chicken and dumplings. The thin version that is similar to chicken noodle soup and the heavier cream sauce version that I have here.

Chicken Gumbo

Recipe Description

The classic creole dish featuring the obligatory holy trinity of peppers, onions, and celery. This is the Cajun version of mirepoix. Gumbo is fantastic in that it is both light and flavorful at the same time. Be careful with the rice. As a little can go a long way. If you put in too much rice, you will end up with a rice dish *(not a soup)* that tastes like gumbo. I have learned this from experience.

Tasting Guidelines

Taste is **savory,** a little spicy, and aromatic.
Weight is **light** but can be balanced with vinegar and tomatoes.
Texture is **soupy.**
For **low to moderate** treatment side effects.
Emotional response of **good ol' Cajun love.**
Best categorized as **Cajun.**

Ingredients

2 lbs. chicken breast, cut into 1/2" chunks
1 c. rice, cooked
1 large can tomatoes
2 green peppers, cored, diced, seeded
1 yellow onion, diced
4 celery stalks, chopped
1 bag okra, frozen
2 large cans chicken broth
oil/butter

Flavor Balancers

kosher salt to taste
black pepper to taste
cayenne pepper
red wine vinegar

Aromatics

2 tbsp. garlic, minced
2 bay leaves

Recipe Directions

Bring a large pot to a medium heat. Add 1 to 2 tbsp. of oil or butter for sautéing. Sauté onions, green peppers, celery, and garlic. Cook until translucent. At this point, stir in chicken breast cut into 1/2" chunks. Sauté chicken until lightly brown and cooked thoroughly. Salt and pepper. After the chicken is done, lightly deglaze the pan with red wine vinegar. Allow to reduce. Stir in tomatoes, chicken broth, and okra. Bring to a boil. Taste and adjust seasonings as needed. Allow to simmer 45 minutes until okra is thoroughly cooked and all flavors are intermingled. Serve immediately in bowls over hot rice.

Chef Tips

This recipe employs what is referred to in Cajun and creole food as "the holy trinity." The Holy Trinity is onions, celery, and green peppers. This forms the base for that traditional Louisiana flavor. Also, see cornbread recipe in the sides section. It goes well with this recipe. Serving the rice on the side keeps the rice from expanding and overly thickening the gumbo.

Chicken Noodle Soup

Recipe Description

An American classic. If there is somebody in the United States that has never heard of chicken noodle soup, they must live under the world's largest rock. This dish is what I consider to be a slightly up-market take on the dish. This chicken noodle features big cuts of veggies, egg noodles, and a good aromatic quality.

Tasting Guidelines

Taste is **savory** and aromatic.

Weight is **light** but can be balanced with sugar and red wine vinegar.

Texture is **soupy.**

For **moderate to severe** treatment side effects.

Emotional response of being **loved when you are sick.**

Best categorized as **classic American.**

Ingredients

1/2 pound chicken breast, cooked and chopped

1 24 oz. pack of egg noodles, cooked

1/2 cup onion, chopped

1/2 cup celery, chopped

1/2 cup carrots, sliced

2 large can chicken broth

1 tbsp. oil

Flavor Balancers

kosher salt to taste

black pepper to taste

1 tbsp. red wine vinegar

1 tbsp. sugar

Aromatics

2 bay leaves

1 tbsp. ground sage

Recipe Directions

Heat oil and 1 c. water in a large spaghetti pot over medium heat. Cook the onion, celery, and carrots until tender allowing the water to reduce and sautéing the vegetables after the water evaporates. Add chicken and sauté lightly as well. Add seasonings and broth. Allow to come to a boil. Reduce from a boil and allow to simmer 30 minutes. Add egg noodles 5 minutes before serving. Remove bay leaves immediately before serving.

Chef Tips

For a more savory soup, add a small can of diced tomatoes, mushrooms, or 1 tbsp. MSG.

For a little kick, add a little cayenne pepper in the beginning of cooking. It will help with any congestion in the head. A little red wine vinegar can help ease a queasy stomach as can a few slices of peeled fresh ginger. Do not eat the slices of ginger, remove before serving.

Chili

Texas Disclaimer

To all the Texans out there: yes, I realize that "real chili" has no beans in it. But the purpose of this recipe is to provide a friendly, well-rounded chili that everyone can enjoy.

Recipe Description

This is a family recipe passed down from my grandfather to me. I have slightly modified it to make it friendlier for chemo and lighter over all. It is a good, all-around chili. It is very versatile and can be eaten as a meal, over pasta, or even over hot dogs if you like. If you feel like your chili might be missing something, I highly recommend adding some ketchup.

Tasting Guidelines

Taste is **savory,** peppery, and a little sweet and tangy.

Weight is **medium** but can be balanced with vinegar and ketchup.

Texture is **soft** and chili like.

For **low to moderate** treatment side effects.

Emotional response of feeling **warm on a cold winters night.**

Best categorized as **classic American.**

Ingredients

1 lb. lean ground beef or ground turkey, *(at least 90/10 or leaner beef)*

2 large cans of chili beans or red kidney beans, undrained

1 large can tomatoes, diced and undrained

2 green peppers, cored and medium diced

1 large onion, medium diced

2 tbsp. canola oil

Flavor Balancers

3 tsp. kosher salt
2 tbsp. soy sauce
1/2 tsp. cayenne pepper
2 tbsp. red wine vinegar
2 tbsp. sugar

Aromatics

2 tbsp. garlic, minced
1 tbsp. cumin, ground
2 tbsp. dried oregano
1 tbsp. chili powder

Recipe Directions

In a large sauté pan or skillet, bring oil to medium heat. Add garlic, onions, and green pepper. Lightly sauté for 5 minutes. Add enough water to lightly cover the ingredients. Cover pan and allow to sweat until onions are translucent.

Break up ground beef. Add to sauté pan, mixing all ingredients together. Cook beef thoroughly and try to keep the ground beef chunks as small as possible. Now you will add the diced tomatoes, black pepper, salt, cumin, chili powder, cayenne pepper, and soy sauce. Cover with water. And allow to simmer and reduce. Similar to how you make homemade tacos.

Reduce liquid until it forms a bit of sauce at the very bottom. If your saute pan is large enough, add remaining ingredients, stirring thoroughly and allowing to simmer on low heat for several hours. If not, transfer to spaghetti pot and repeat above method. For ease and convenience, I like my chili to simmer in a slow cooker so I don't burn it.

The idea here is the longer the flavors sit together, the better they taste. Serve with your favorite chili condiments, like oyster crackers, sour dough bread bowl, freshly chopped onions, cheddar cheese, hot sauce, etc. Whatever you like or whatever your chemo patient is able to eat.

Chef Tips

If chili is heavy, add red wine vinegar and sugar to lighten the flavor.

SMOOTHIES

Smoothies are amazing! The flavor combinations are literally endless. They are great for sneaking super healthy things into your body with out you even noticing. What I love about smoothies is they can be simple and flavorful. They can also be engineered to act as an entire meal replacement. Smoothies are also great as snacks or as a substitute for a heavy meal when you have severe mouth sores.

The way I think about smoothies is the way I think about ice cream. Whatever flavor combinations of ice cream you like, are naturally going to be the flavors of smoothies you like. For example, I personally love chocolate ice cream! So one of my favorite smoothie flavor combinations is chocolate, strawberry, and banana.

Another great thing about smoothies is the ability to add dietary supplements. You can add whey proteins, multivitamins, or meal replacement shakes, like muscle milk, to increase the nutritional value. A chain of businesses that has capitalized on this idea is a brand called, Smoothie King. If you are ever lacking on ideas, visit one of their stores or website to get some inspiration. Or, you can just buy one of their delicious smoothies.

Palate Cleansing With Smoothies

To properly do a palate cleanse when cooking, we normally use red wine vinegar to remove metallic taste and lighten the weight of a dish. In smoothies, we want to use citrus juices instead of vinegar. Examples of this would be lemons, limes, and oranges. The citric acid helps cut through the metallic taste. Its acidity helps to leave a clean feeling in your mouth.

A great example of a smoothie that uses this technique would be a mango and lime smoothie.

General Smoothie Directions

1) Add all ingredients into the blender and cover.

2) Activate the blender. If you have frozen ingredients that are not cooperating, use the pulse function and a little finesse to pulse your way into the perfect mixture.

3) Taste your smoothie and adjust. Is there too much strawberry? Is there not enough chocolate? Is the smoothie too tart because you used Greek yogurt instead of regular yogurt? Adjust the flavors just like you would do anything else.

4)Serve in a glass, preferably with a straw. Garnish if desired.

Smoothie vs. Milkshake

The difference between a smoothie and a milkshake is simple but fundamental. A milkshake is partially melted ice cream with flavorings suspended with in its structure that has been thinned enough to be presented in a drinkable form. A smoothie is a drinkable, partially frozen liquid, that may or may not contain yogurt. It is generally made out of blended fruit and ice. In simple terms, a milkshake is basically melted ice cream where as a smoothie is blended fruit with ice in a drinkable form.

Supplements

Supplements are a great way to work certain necessary dietary items into a meal that you may or may not be getting originally. Supplements could be something as simple as sneaking kale, spinach, or vegetable juice into the smoothie. Supplements could also be specific vitamins or minerals: like B12, potassium, calcium, and other dietary supplements.

Last but not least, supplements can also include meal replacement or performance type supplements. Examples of this would be: Slim Fast, Ensure, Muscle Milk, whey protein, Creatine, and many other sports oriented supplements.

What you put into your smoothies as supplements should be something you discuss with your doctor or registered dietitian. They will be able to guide you more thoroughly in creating a more effective meal replacement strategy then anything I could ever hope to write in this book.

Remember, when you make smoothies, it is like anything else. You want to create a well-rounded meal. A general rule of thumb would be to make certain you are making smoothies that contain vitamins, minerals, carbohydrates, fats, and proteins. This is especially true if the focus is to use these smoothies as meal replacements.

Prepping and Storing Ingredients

If you are pressed for time, you can always prep your smoothie meal a head of time so when you are hungry you can just blend and drink.

There are many ways to make your life easier. One easy way is simply portioning the ingredients into food storage bags and either refrigerating or freezing them. You can portion them for an entire day or even for the week.

For yogurt, you can simply take an ice cube tray, fill it with yogurt, and freeze it. After the yogurt is frozen, you can add the yogurt cubes to your pre-portioned freezer bags. If that is too much extra work, you can always just add the yogurt to the blender when you are ready to make the smoothie.

For storage of ingredients, you always want to make sure everything is properly prepared and sealed to prevent any cross-contamination or food poisoning. I used mostly frozen fruits for my mom while she was going through chemo. Because there is no safe way to decontaminate fresh fruits and vegetables, using frozen fruits and vegetables lowers the risk of accidentally getting food poisoning. If you have any further questions, feel free to reference the *Food Safety* chapter.

In closing, feel free to play around with the following smoothie recipes. Don't be afraid to Google other recipes and try them out. The smoothie recipes in this book are only a frame of reference and a starting point for you to begin. Enjoy!

Strawberry-Banana Smoothie

Ingredients

1 scoop chocolate protein powder

1/2 c. milk

1/4 c. of honey vanilla Greek yogurt

5 frozen strawberries

1 ripe banana

2 tbsp. sugar

1/2 c. ice cubes

Carrot Pineapple Smoothie

Ingredients

1 c. carrots, steamed and thoroughly cooked until soft and then chilled

2 c. canned pineapple, chopped

1 ripe banana

1/2 c. orange juice

1/2 c. ice

Kiwi Orange and Apple Smoothie

Ingredients

8 kiwifruit, peeled

2 apples, peeled and cored

1 c. orange juice

1 tbsp. sugar

1/2 c. ice

Chocolate Peanut Butter Banana Shake

Ingredients

1 scoop chocolate protein powder
1/4 c. creamy peanut butter
1/4 c. milk
1/2 c. honey Greek yogurt
2 ripe bananas
1 tbsp. sugar
1/2 c. ice cubes

Blueberry and Pineapple Smoothie

Ingredients

1/2 c. honey Greek yogurt
1/2 c. frozen blueberries
1 c. canned pineapple, chopped
2 tbsp. sugar
1/2 c. ice cubes

Blueberry Lemon Smoothie

Ingredients

1 c. vanilla Greek yogurt
1/2 c. frozen blueberries
juice of one lemon

Strawberry Mango Smoothie

Ingredients

1 c. honey Greek yogurt

1 c. frozen strawberries

1 mango

1/2 c. sugar

Mango Cherry Smoothie

Ingredients

1/2 c. honey Greek yogurt

1 mango, peeled

8 cherries, seeds and stems removed

1/4 c. orange juice

1/2 c. sugar

Mai Tai Smoothie

Ingredients

1 c. honey Greek yogurt

1 c. canned pineapple, cubed

2 seedless oranges, peeled

4 maraschino cherries or 4 fresh seedless cherries and 2 tbsp. grenadine

1/4 c. sugar

1/2 c. ice

Strawberry Smoothie

Ingredients

1/4 c. milk
1 c. honey Greek yogurt
2 c. frozen strawberries
2 tbsp. sugar
1/2 c. ice

Banana Smoothie

Ingredients

1/4 c. milk
1 c. honey Greek yogurt
4 ripe bananas
2 tbsp. sugar
1/2 c. ice

Bananas Foster Smoothie

Ingredients

1/4 c. milk
1 c. honey Greek yogurt
4 ripe bananas
2 tbsp. maple syrup
2 tsp. cinnamon
2 tbsp. sugar
1/2 c. ice

SUPPLEMENTAL GUIDES

Standard and Metric Measurement Conversions

These are some handy charts for referencing different measurements. This so that you can increase your recipes, decrease your recipes, or convert them to metric if you do not use USA standard measurements. Converting recipes is actually very easy once you understand the basics of measurement. American recipes use fluid measurements for most household recipes, even for dry ingredients. If you live outside of the United States you can always pick up a set of American measuring cups and measuring spoons off of Amazon.com for your convenience.

Fluid Measurements

Standard Name	Abbreviations	Milliliters	Ounces (Fluid)	Components
1 Teaspoon	t., tsp., tsp.s.	5ml	.1667 ounces	None
1 Tablespoon	T., Tbsp.	15 ml	.5 ounces	3 Teaspoons
1 Cup	C, Cp.	240 ml	8 ounces	16 Tablespoons
1 Pint	P., Pt.	480 ml	16 ounces	2 Cups
1 Quart	Q., Qt.	960 ml	32 ounces	2 Pints
1 Gallon	G., Gal.	3840 ml	128 ounces	4 Quarts

Weight Measurements

Standard Name	Abbreviations	Converted	Components
1 Ounce	O., Oz.	28.35 grams	None
1 Pound	Lb., Lbs., #	453.59 grams	16 Ounces
1 Gram	g., gm.	0.035 ounces	1000 Milligrams
1 Kilogram	Kg., kgm.	2.2 pounds	1000 Grams

Temperature Measurements

Fahrenheit	Celsius	Significance of Temperature
0	-18	Long Term Freezer Storage
32	0	Freezing Water
40	5	Refrigerator Temperature
145	63	Seafood and Veggies Cooked, Ready to Eat Foods Temp.
155	69	Beef, and Red Meats Well-Done Temperature
165	74	Chicken, Turkey, Poultry Well-Done Temperature
212	100	Boiling Water
300	149	Low Bake Temperature
350	177	Medium Bake Temperature
375	191	Medium-High Bake Temp
400	205	High Bake Temperature
425	219	Roasting Temperature
450	233	High Roasting Temperature.

These temperatures are the direct conversions from Fahrenheit to Celsius. Feel free to convert them into easier to use versions that are more appropriate to your region.

Specialty Measurements

1 Pinch is the amount of seasoning you can pick up between your thumb and forefinger
1 Dash is roughly equivalent to 3 pinches
1 Stick of Butter = 4 ounces or 113.34 grams. In the US butter is sold by the pound, but each pound is broken up into long thin quarters that we call "sticks."
1 Cup of Flour weighs 120 grams when measured correctly.

British English to American English Concept Conversion Chart

Because the English speaking world is spread across many continents with local variations at each turn, I have provided the following concept conversion chart. Hopefully this concept conversion chart can help my international readers understand what each ingredient is! This should also help anyone who wants to use recipes from other English speaking countries.

A Big Thanks to wearenotfoodies.com for making this list of food terms used in the UK and their American Equivalents!

This list was sourced from: http://wearenotfoodies.com/

British English	American English	Notes
Aubergine	Eggplant	
Beetroot	Beet	
Bacon	Bacon	In the UK, bacon is predominantly from the back of the pig, while in the US it is from the belly, which in the UK is called streaky
Bain Marie	Double Boiler	
Banger	Sausage	
Bilberry	Blueberry	
Biscuit	Cookie	
Boiled Sweet	Hard Candy	
Broad Bean	Fava	
Candy Floss	Cotton Candy	
Caster Sugar	Superfine Sugar	
Chicory	Endive	This applies to Belgian endive only
Chipolata	Cocktail Sausage	
Chips	French Fries	
Chili con Carne	Chili	
Chili Sauce	Hot Sauce	
Cider	Hard Cider	
Clingfilm	Plastic Wrap	
Conserves	Preserves	

Coriander	Cilantro	In the UK coriander means both the spice and the herb, where-as in the US it just means the spice.
Cornflour	Cornstarch	
Cos lettuce	Romaine lettuce	
Courgette	Zucchini or Summer Squash	
Cream, Double	Heavy Cream	
Cream, Single	Half and half	
Crisps	Chips	
Cutlery	Flatware or Silverware	
Cutlet	Chop	
Demerara sugar	Light brown cane sugar	
Digestive Biscuit	Graham cracker	Though not the same, they can be used interchangeably in recipes as they have a similar taste
Fairycake	Cupcake	
Fillet Steak	Filet mignon or Tenderloin	
Fish Fingers	Fish Sticks	
French Beans	String Beans/Green Beans	
Frying Pan	Skillet	
Gammon	Ham	
Glace Fruits	Candied Fruits	
Greaseproof Paper	Wax Paper	
Green / Red Peppers	Bell Peppers	
Grill	Broiler	
Hull	Shuck	
Hundreds and Thousands	Sprinkles	
Ice lolly	Popsicle	
Icing	Frosting	
Icing Sugar	Confectioner's Sugar	
Jam	Jelly	
Jelly	Jell-o	
Kipper	Smoked Herring	
Lemonade	Lemonade	In the UK lemonade is a fizzy soda drink while in the US it is traditional lemonade made from water, sugar and real lemons.
Liquidizer	Blender	

Main Course	Entrée	The word Entrée is sometimes used in the UK, but for an appetizer
Mangetout	Snow peas	
Mince	Ground	as in ground beef
Muesli	Granola	
Pastry case	Pie case	
Paw Paw	Papaya	Papaya is also commonly used in the UK
Pie	Pot Pie	The word pie in the UK predominantly means a savoury pie usually filled with meat
Plain flour	All-purpose flour	
Porridge	Oatmeal, Cooked	
Prawn	Small Shrimp	
Profiterole	Cream Puff	
Pudding	Dessert	
Rocket	Arugula	
Rump steak	Sirloin	
Scone	Biscuit	Similar but not quite the same
Self-raising flour	Self-rising flour	
Semolina	Cream of wheat	
Sirloin	Porterhouse	
Soft Drink,Pop, Fizzy Juice	Soda, Pop, Soda Pop, Coke, many more	
Sorbet	Sherbert	
Spirit	Liquor	
Spring Onions	Green Onions	Scallions is another term that is sometimes used in both countries
Stone	Pit	as in peaches
Sultanas	Golden Raisins	
Swede	Rutabaga	Also known as a yellow turnip and in Scotland these are called Neeps
Sweet	Dessert	
Sweetcorn (maize)	Corn	
Sweets	Candy	
Tart	Pie	In the UK pies have lids and are savoury, tarts don't have lids and are sweet

Tin Foil	Aluminum Foil	
Tinned	Canned	
Toffee	Taffy	
Treacle	Molasses	
Wholemeal flour	Whole-wheat flour	

Herbs and Spices Chart
Flavor, Function, When to add them, and Common Uses

Herb/Spice	Flavor/ Function	Common Uses
Anise (Spice)	**Flavor:** Licorice flavor **Function:** Warming. Add in beginning of a dish.	Mediterranean cuisine, Middle Eastern cuisine, Chinese cuisine, Indian cuisine, Vietnamese cuisine, fish, cakes, cookies, breads, stews
Allspice (Spice)	**Flavor:** Pepper with notes of cinnamon, nutmeg and cloves. **Function:** Rounded, spiced flavor. Add in the beginning of a dish.	beef, chicken, curries, fruits, ginger, Jamaican cuisine, meats, pumpkin, squash
Basil (Herb)	**Flavor:** Sweet with a hint of licorice. **Function:** Adds freshness to a dish. Add at the very end of a dish. Absolutely last.	bell peppers, cheese, chicken, eggplant, eggs, fish, garlic, Italian cuisine, lamb, lemon, meats, Mediterranean cuisine, mint, olive oil, oregano, pasta, pesto, pizza, salads, salmon, salt, shellfish, soups, Thai cuisine, tomatoes, tomato sauces, vegetables, vinegar, watermelon, zucchini
Bay Leaves (Herb)	**Flavor:** sweet **Function:** Adds richness and savory to dishes. Add in the beginning to give time to work throughout the dish.	beans, fish, meats, parsley, rice, soups, stews, stocks and broths, thyme, tomatoes and tomato sauces
Caraway Seeds (Spice)	**Flavor:** sweet, sour **Function:** Adds zest. Add at the beginning of dish or baking.	breads (esp. pumpernickel and rye), cheese, German cuisine, pork, potatoes, sauerkraut
Cardamom (Spice)	**Flavor:** sweet, pungent **Function:** Adds heating effect. Add at the beginning of a dish.	chicken, cinnamon, coffee, coriander, curries, dates, desserts, ginger, Indian cuisine, lamb, oranges, rice, tea
Cayenne Pepper (Spice)	**Flavor:** spicy **Function:** Adds spiciness to a dish. Add at the beginning of a dish.	bell peppers, Cajun cuisine, fish, tomatoes
Chives (Herb)	**Flavor:** green onion **Function:** Adds light onion flavor to dishes. Added at the end.	cheese, eggs, parsley, pork, potatoes, salads, sauces, soups, sour cream, tarragon, vegetables

Cilantro (Fresh Coriander Leaves) (Herb)	**Flavor:** sweet, sour, citrus **Function:** Adds a cooling note to spicy dishes and a freshness to dishes. Add at the very very end. Mostly used as a garnish.	Asian cuisines, avocados, chicken, chile peppers, coconut, cumin, curries, fish, garlic, ginger, Indian cuisine, lemon, lemongrass, lime, Mexican cuisine, mint, rice, salads, salsas, tacos, Thai cuisine, tomatoes, yogurt
Cinnamon (Spice)	**Flavor:** sweet, bitter, pungent **Function:** Adds warmth to dishes. Add in the beginning of a dish. Needs time to work in and mellow.	apples, baked dishes and goods, bananas, hot beverages, blueberries, breakfast/brunch, chicken, chocolate, coffee, cloves, curries, custards, desserts, fruits, garam masala, ginger, lamb, lemon, Mexican cuisine, Middle Eastern cuisine, Moroccan cuisine, mulled wine nutmeg, oranges, pears, pecans, pork, rice, sugar, tea, vanilla
Cloves (Spice)	**Flavor:** sweet, pungent **Function:** Adds warmth to dishes. Add in the beginning of a dish.	apples, chocolate, cinnamon, garam masala, ginger, ham, lemon, mulled wine, oranges, pork
Coriander (Spice)	**Flavor:** sour, pungent, dry **Function:** Cools dish's flavors. Add in the middle of cooking a dish.	chicken, chile peppers, citrus, crab, cumin, curries, fish, garlic, lentils, pepper, pork
Cumin (Spice)	**Flavor:** bitter, sweet **Function:** Heating of dishes. Add in the middle of cooking a dish or early if used in a marinade. It needs time to de-funkify.	beans, chickpeas, coriander, couscous, curries, eggplant, garlic, Indian cuisine, lamb, lentils, Mexican cuisine, Moroccan cuisine, pork, potatoes, rice, sausages, tomatoes
Curry Powder (Spice Blend)	**Flavor:** bittersweet, pungent **Function:** Adds aromatic quality to dishes. Add early to a dish. Needs time to mellow.	ginger, Indian cuisine, Thai cuisine, vegetables
Dill (Herb)	**Flavor:** sour, sweet **Function:** Adds freshness to dishes. Add at the very end of a dish. It is a delicate herb.	beets, cabbage, carrots, cilantro, cucumbers, eggs, fish, parsley, pickles, potatoes, salads, salmon
Fennel (Spice)	**Flavor:** sweet **Function:** It adds a licorice sweetness to dishes. Add midway through cooking a dish.	Chinese cuisine, fish, five spice powder, Italian cuisine, pork, sausages, shellfish

Garlic (Root Vegetable)	**Flavor:** Aromatic, touch of spicy **Function:** Adds warmth to dishes. Always add the very beginning of a dish. **Chef Note:** There are very few applications that cannot be benefited by the addition of garlic.	basil, cheese, chicken, chinese cuisine, French cuisine, Indian cuisine, Italian cuisine, Korean cuisine, lamb, lemon, meats, Mediterranean cuisine, Mexican cuisine, Middle Eastern cuisine, Moroccan cuisine, mushrooms, mustard, olive oil, onions, salt, tomatoes, Vietnamese cuisine, vinegars
Ginger (Spice)	**Flavor:** sour and hot **Function:** Adds warmth to dishes. **Chef Note:** Great for an upset stomach! Add at the beginning of a dish if you want it to mellow. Add towards the end if you want it to add a pop of flavor.	apples, asian cuisine, basil, beverages
Marjoram (Herb)	**Flavor:** Sweet and spicy and in the same family as oregano, just lighter in flavor. **Function:** Adds a light, crisp peppery-ness. Add in the middle of a dish.	basil, cheese-goat mozzarella, Italian Cuisine, Greek Cuisine
Mint (Herb)	**Flavor:** sweet crisp herb **Function:** It adds a subtle, cleansing pop. Like basil add at end of cooking so you don't lose its pop. **Chef's Note:** Mint is also known to calm your stomach. Add at the very end of a dish. The flavor is very delicate.	beverages, chocolate, cream, ice cream, desserts, teas
Nutmeg (Spice)	**Flavor:** Aromatic spice. Typically used in fall and winter dishes. **Function:** To add a sense of warmth to a dish. Add to food in the beginning. If adding to drinks, add at the end as a topper.	apples, cheese, chicken, cream/milk, desserts, eggnog, lamb, pasta and pasta sauces, puddings, rice, veal
Oregano (Herb)	**Flavor:** Rich, aromatic, and peppery herb. **Function:** It adds a nice, subtle black pepper flavor that blends well with food. Add at the beginning of a dish to give it time to work through the dish.	beans, beef, chicken, fish, lamb, meats, pasta and pasta sauces, salads, soups

Paprika (Spice)	**Flavor:** Sweet-hot, depending on variety. **Function:** It adds a very light touch of warmth and heat. Due to its muted and subtle flavor, it is mainly used to add color to a dish. Add at the very end.	beef, chicken, eggs, fish, pork
Parsley (Herb)	**Flavor:** It's bitter and fresh. **Function:** To be used as a pallet cleanser. Add at the very end. Always put on top. You never want to cook it into a dish. **Chef's Note:** Flat leaf aka Italian parsley is fantastic to use in dishes where you need a freshness and a crispness. Parsley is also fantastic for cleansing palates. How this relates to chemotherapy nutrition is leaves your mouth feeling clean and fresh after every bite, which in turn with make a heavy dish feel light. This is especially important for people who have had trouble eating healthy foods.	basil, carrots, chicken, eggplant, fish, pasta and pasta sauces, pork, potatoes, soups, stews, stocks, vegetables
Pepper, Black (Spice)	**Flavor:** It's mildly spicy and warm. **Function:** The most basic spice to fill out a flavor profile with. Add in the beginning of a dish.	beef, eggs, game, meats/red, salt, steaks
Poppy Seeds (Spice)	**Flavor:** sweet and aromatic **Function:** Used mainly in baked goods to add a fun floral aroma. Usually added before baking baked goods.	breads, cakes, cookies, butter, cheese, pasta, potatoes, salads and salad dressings, zucchini
Red Pepper (Spice)	**Flavor:** hot **Function:** Adds spiciness and heat to a dish. Add in small increments in the beginning of a dish. meats, seafood	
Rosemary (Herb)	**Flavor:** An aromatic herb adds a rich warmth to dishes. **Function:** Add early in cooking to add a rich warmth and depth to your dishes.	beans, breads, butter, chicken, duck, fish, lamb

Sage (Herb)	**Flavor:** Highly aromatic. It is the single ingredient that makes everything it is in smell like Thanksgiving. **Function:** Add last in cooking to add warmth and depth to the dish.	stuffing, turkey, poultry, traditional American food
Savory (Herb)	**Flavor:** Savory is exactly like it sounds, savory. Its flavor is a blend between thyme, rosemary, and sage. **Function:** It adds savoriness and aromatic quality to a dish. Add early in cooking.	beans, beef, chicken, garlic, red meat, starchy potatoes, tomatoes
Tarragon (Herb)	**Flavor:** Its flavor is like liquorice, heavier than basil but lighter than normal liquorice flavor. **Function:** It adds lightness and freshness to a dish. Add last to a dish.	acidic foods, poultry, eggs, fish, light flavored dishes
Thyme (Herb)	**Flavor:** aromatic and rich **Function:** Adds warmth to dishes and gives food a wholesome taste. Add about midway through the dish.	marinara sauce, tomatoes, red meats, poultry, roasted meats, starchy vegetables
Turmeric (Spice)	**Flavor:** It's the main spice in curry. It is the spice that gives seasoned salt its flavor. **Function:** Warms up a dish. Add in the beginning or middle of cooking a dish.	chicken, curries, indian cuisine, Middle Eastern cuisine, Moroccan cuisine, pork, rice, Thai cuisine

Parts of this list, uses, and descriptions were researched from: The Flavor Bible by Karen Page and Andrew Dornenburg. For a great reference on flavors, seasonings, and ingredients, this book is a fantastic advanced class on the subjects.

Reference Page

Books

The Complete Mediterranean Cookbook
By Tess Mallos

The Flavor Bible
By Karen Page and Andrew Bornenburg

The Wok
A complete and easy guide to preparing a wide variety of authentic Chinese favorites.
By Gary Lee

On Cooking
A textbook of culinary fundamentals
By Sarah R. Labensky and Alan M. Hause

Joy of Cooking
By Rombauer, Becker, Becker

Websites

usda.gov
smithsonianmag.com
blogs.scientificamerican.com
health.harvard.edu
sciencedirect.com
m.ajcn.nutrition.org
medicinenet.com
mayoclinic.org

Connect With Us

Website

www.cookingforchemo.org

Twitter

@cookingforchemo

Facebook

facebook.com/cookingforchemo

Pinterest

pinterest.com/cookingforchemo

Instagram

@chef_ryan_callahan

About The Author

Chef Ryan Callahan is the author of *Cooking for Chemo ...and After!*, *Cooking for Kids with Cancer*, *Cooking for Cancer and After*, and *Chef Ryan Callahan's Tasting Journal.*

Chef Ryan won a 2016 Gourmand World Cookbook Award for his groundbreaking book *Cooking for Chemo ...and After!*

He is a hospitality industry veteran with over 15 years of hands on culinary experience.

Chef Ryan is currently focused on teaching the cancer and chemotherapy community how to think, act, and cook like a true chef.

The cooking techniques contained within his books were developed after he became his mother's primary caregiver during her battle with breast cancer. His years of culinary experience combined with this unique hands on learning opportunity created the ground breaking ideas first discussed in *Cooking for Chemo ...and After!*

Made in the USA
Middletown, DE
13 April 2022

64202597R00137